Hatch, Robert

The Hero Project: 2
Teen, 1 Notebook, 13
Extraordinary Inter-
views

3/08

The Hero Project

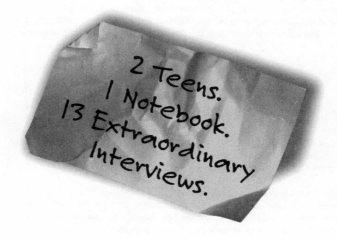

2 Teens.
1 Notebook.
13 Extraordinary
Interviews.

Robert Hatch and William Hatch

McGraw-Hill

New York Chicago San Francisco Lisbon London Madrid Mexico City
Milan New Delhi San Juan Seoul Singapore Sydney Toronto

Library of Congress Cataloging-in-Publication Data

Hatch, Robert.
    The hero project : how we met our greatest heroes and what we learned from them
/ by Robert Hatch and William Hatch.
        p.   cm.
    ISBN 0-07-144904-3 (alk. paper)
      1. Heroes—Biography.   2. Biography—20th century.   I. Hatch, William.
II. Title.

CT120.H36   2006
920'.009'04—dc22   2005017518

1 2 3 4 5 6 7 8 9 0   FGR/FGR   0 9 8 7 6 5

ISBN 0-07-144904-3

Photographs on pages 1, 31, 51, 73, 91, 105, 121, 135, 149, 165, and 187 courtesy of AP
Worldwide Photos; photograph on page 17 courtesy of Sigrid Estrada; photograph on
page 61 courtesy of Henderson Photography

This book is printed on acid-free paper.

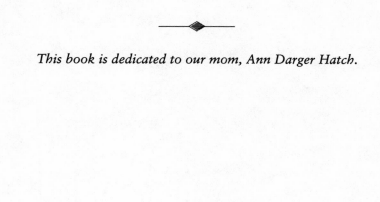

This book is dedicated to our mom, Ann Darger Hatch.

Contents

Foreword

◆

In an age when we are led to believe that the young people in our country think only about movies, magazines, and malls and don't give a thought to who might be their heroes outside of the current rock stars, this book is a great wake-up call. As you read about the truly incredible process these two brothers have gone through as they first conceived a list of people who were their heroes and then believed that they could actually interview them—one on one—you will realize that there are also very real heroes in the Hatch family! They will make you smile at their dogged persistence and ingenuity, and you will marvel at parents who encouraged them and were willing to drop everything and do whatever it took to get these kids to interviews with true celebrities of international fame—people whom we would consider unreachable on a face-to-face basis, even in our wildest dreams, such as Desmond Tutu, Lance Armstrong, Yo-Yo Ma, and Jimmy Carter.

Lest you think they went into this without much thought, you will see that they did their homework. All the information available to them about each person was carefully read and digested (and is included in this book before each interview) so that when they were actually eyeball to eyeball with each hero, they were ready with a list of insightful and educated questions—sometimes questions that many of us adults would love to have answered but would never dare ask—that they asked without a qualm. And the answers are fascinating.

How proud we are of these friends of ours! In our writing and speaking over the past twenty years, we have been saying that one of the greatest things children can have in their quest for success in life is heroes. Heroes give them something to reach for and emulate as they find their own way to get where they want to be. We have found in raising nine children of our own that if goals for our children are *ours* as parents, they don't go very far. As soon as the goals become *theirs* through a real desire to accomplish great things as they see qualities they want to emulate in their heroes, the chances of success are profoundly higher.

In order to appreciate this book fully, you need to know a bit about this remarkable Hatch family, which includes six children. Both parents, Ann and Randy, have been educated at Columbia University and are excellent writers and journalists in their own right. As friends and neighbors we have observed that the journey of life for this delightfully dynamic family has not been an easy one. In many ways their journey has resembled the wild ride of a NASCAR race as both parents have dealt with brain tumors—one operable and one not. They have watched their house be destroyed by fire and have experienced the joy as well as the sorrows of having a youngest child with Down syndrome. Through it all, they have been supported by magnificent grandparents who have given all of them the power to go on. No, their life journey could not really be described as a luxury cruise. Rather it is like a cruise that stops at faraway and exotic destinations; they have somehow managed to arrive at fascinating places with voice recorder and thoughtful questions in hand to interview people who have changed the world in their own field of passion.

For Will and Rob, who possess undying creative determination and resilience, the question was not *if* I get the interview but *when and how* should I do it. Through a process of twelve years and persistent, consistent requests, they have experienced many disappointments as well as successes. They have had their hopes dashed over and over again, yet, undaunted, they pressed on and have now produced a truly remarkable book that will delight young and old alike.

Both the words on the page and the sheer determination it required to get them there by both young men as well as their parents inspire all of us, including this very gifted new generation of youth, to think about these heroes as well as to compile a list of our own and to help us all to accomplish one of life's greatest goals: a passion for excellence!

—RICHARD AND LINDA EYRE,
authors of the number-one *New York Times*
bestseller *Teaching Your Children Values*

Acknowledgments

This project could never have happened without the help of lots of kind people. Our dad, Randy Hatch, accompanied us to all of the early interviews. Our mom, Ann Darger Hatch, and grandma Arlene Darger transcribed the interviews and proofed the chapters before we sent them to the publisher. Our uncle Jeff Hatch forwarded us the money to get to one of the interviews. Our brothers Jake Pollard and George and Spence Hatch went with us to some of the later interviews. Many many thanks to Sarah Pollard, J. Rordam, and Julia Parker Hatch for letting us bounce ideas off them ad nauseum.

And then there are all the people who were willing to go out of their way to help us contact a hero. Many thanks to all of them, and especially to our aunt Jan Denali, Senator Orrin Hatch as well as his staff, Mary Ann Lee of Children's Dance Theater, Paul Fireman of Reebok, Peggy Fletcher Stack of the *Salt Lake Tribune*, Solon So and Willie Chan of the JC Group, Camilla Chavez, Thomas S. Monson of the Church of Jesus Christ of Latter-day Saints, the late Christopher Reeve, Steve Covey, the late Senator Ted Moss, our grandpa George C. Hatch, Senator Robert Bennett, Al Joyner, our aunt Frances Darger, the promotion department of the Hansen Planetarium, Richard and Linda Eyre, Rabbi Harold Kushner, our grandpa Stanford P. Darger, Justice Sandra Day O'Connor, and Richard Bizarro, formerly of Weider Nutrition.

Introduction

This project started about twelve years ago. My family was living in Ogden, Utah. I was dancing with Children's Dance Theater, which is a professional modern dance company in Salt Lake City, Utah. Folk singer Pete Seeger came to do a concert with us, and both of my parents freaked out. They kept telling me what an amazing thing it was for me to be able to be around this man, that he had helped to change history in many good ways, and that he was a legend and a hero of theirs. To me he looked like a tall, skinny old man who was a little forgetful.

But I liked watching him. I started noticing the songs that he'd written over the past fifty years (songs like "Where Have All the Flowers Gone?" and "If I Had a Hammer") and noticing the kinds of ideas that he talked about in his songs. I liked the ballads that he'd sing about people who stood up for what they believed in, and I liked his songs about protecting the earth.

So I wrote him a couple of letters. And he wrote me back, which is extraordinary in itself! When I told him that my parents thought he was a hero, he said that he wasn't. He wrote, "You've heard of the statement, 'All idols have feet of clay.' I make mistakes, and I hope you don't try to make—I hope *nobody* tries to make—a hero out of me."

I thought that was really interesting. Anyway, Seeger suggested that I think about who my own heroes were and write to them. So I did. It took a few weeks of thinking and reading and asking my friends and my family what they thought.

Along the way, I noticed that kids don't seem to have any heroes. Oh, if I ask my three-year-old nephew who his hero is, he has no hesitation and will tell you that it's Batman. But that isn't even a real person. And as people get older they seem to stop having even fictional people that they look up to and admire and want to be like.

I'll bet that I asked a couple of hundred middle-school kids about their heroes. A few of them named someone that was long dead, like Abraham Lincoln or Martin Luther King. But most of them couldn't think of anyone to name. Some of them named a professional athlete, but they admitted that it was the person's skill playing the game that they admired, not anything about the player himself.

And then O. J. Simpson got into his trouble with the law. I think that a lot of people, and not just people our age, were very shocked that someone who is big, handsome, rich, and very successful could be accused of and tried for murdering his children's mother.

It made me, and my friends, wonder if it was even possible to *be* a hero today, or if our world has become so complicated and selfish that noble behavior isn't possible or can never meet with success.

So I tried to identify some people that I think are heroic. I looked for people with these characteristics:

- Are still alive
- Have made enough money that they don't have to worry about it anymore
- Have overcome unusual hardships
- Behave nobly and unselfishly and are actively involved in giving something back to the community or passing on what they've learned so other people can benefit
- Have made all of our lives better

It seems like a pretty good definition of hero to me. As you read about these people, you might see if you agree with both my definition of hero and with my choices to fill that role.

The group that I came up with is not exactly the same group that is in this book. John Candy was one of this group, and of course he died. Many others declined to be interviewed. I had a couple of basketball players on my first list and wrote to them a few times. But as time went on, they seemed less heroic to me. They were still great athletes, but I didn't see that they were giving much back to other people yet. Maybe it's just that they are still kind of young. Maybe being a hero means that you've lived a long time and have had lots of different experiences to shape the kind of person you are. Most of the heroes I decided on in the end are older.

Anyway, I started writing letters to each of my heroes. Just getting addresses to write to was a real challenge. I spent a lot of time at the library looking in reference books for addresses. It seemed like every book I looked in listed a different address from the one I'd found before. I looked in telephone directories and actually found a couple of them that way. Of course, the job became somewhat easier when my family got Internet access.

You may have heard of a theory called "six degrees of separation." It is the notion that anyone on the planet can be connected to any other person on the planet through a chain of acquaintances that has no more than five intermediaries. In other words, everyone on earth is separated from anyone else by no more than six degrees of separation, or six friends of friends of friends. I tested out that theory. I let all my relatives know what I was doing, hoping that one of them would know someone, who knew someone, who knew one of the heroes.

All in all, I wrote hundreds of letters. I hardly ever got a letter back. I realize that each one of these heroes is doing very important things with their time and that lots of people write them letters and they might not be able to answer each one. It was still a bit frustrating.

Finally my dad sat down with the phone and was eventually able to arrange interviews with some of them. In some of the cases I continued writing letters and Dad kept bothering the agent on the phone for more than two years before we were finally granted an interview or told definitely that the person was not interested in participating.

Without exception, when I met each hero, they were friendly and nice and didn't act at all like I expected a famous person to behave. They seemed so normal—as if they could be a neighbor down the street—that it was easy to forget just how extraordinary each one of these individuals is.

Obviously heroes don't have to be people who are famous. I think that I know some people in my life that are real heroes. But I figured that you probably wouldn't pay money for a book to read about my

Uncle Matt or my neighbor Sharon Webb! So I chose people that you've probably heard of and will enjoy learning more about.

It turns out that books take a lot of years to write. I'm now twenty-three years old, going to college, working full-time and more, and married to a wonderful woman, and my life is very full. I still think a lot about heroes, but I stopped writing the letters several years ago, so the project just sat there.

Five years ago I finally suggested to my younger brother Rob that he take over the whole book project, which he did. He and I even went together to meet Lance Armstrong, and I liked being involved in it again. Rob has identified some great heroes to add to our list.

As I look at all the heroes Rob and I talked to, I'm impressed with the pervading joy they each have in what they do. Some of them are celebrities. Some are not. That has very little to do with their personal heroism. These are people who are worth reading about, people of great productive achievement. It's interesting to me how many of them were from homes of great poverty. I know that I've always had access to electricity, plumbing, and central heating. I know my parents and grandparents have, too. I'm pretty sure even my great-grandparents did. Yet many of these heroes didn't. Did that make them fight harder for their dreams?

Of course, others of these heroes came from homes of privilege, which included private schools and extensive travel. And they, too, achieved their dreams. Some were from huge and close extended families, and others were the only child of a single parent. All of them came from loving and supportive families. That is something they all have in common. And, as I mentioned, all show an overwhelming joy in what they are doing.

So here are the interviews. I'd be interested in hearing from you about your reactions to this book. The publishers have promised that they will send to me any letters that they receive addressed to me. You could also e-mail Rob or me at theheroproject@comcast.net.

I hope you enjoy the book!

—WILL HATCH

Sample Letter

◆

Ms. Madeleine L'Engle
c/o Farrar, Straus and Giroux
19 Union Square West
New York, New York 10003

Dear Ms. L'Engle,

I am a real fan of your children's and adolescent books. I have read everything that you've written (except for a couple of books that Mom says I need to wait a year or two for because I'm just eleven, and they deal with stuff I don't need to know about yet). Many of them I have read several times. Each time that I read one I find new things to appreciate and understand. I like the strong women characters that you create. I like the courage that your kid characters show, even when things look very hopeless and grim. I like how the brothers and sisters are good friends and stick up for each other, and I like it that the kids are often too smart, and not into athletics, and they are still the heroes.

I am a member of the Mormon Church, so I like your images of time and other worlds and the importance each person has in this universe. They feel right to me.

I am eleven years old and am in sixth grade. Until July I lived in Utah, but we moved up to my grandparents' cabin near Yellowstone while my dad is looking for a job. He used to be the publisher of a newspaper. I like living here. The snow is about four feet deep. Sometimes we have to ride the snowmobile to be able to get to the school bus. We are right on a little river, and geese and swans come here for the winter.

I know that you are very busy, and I'm sorry to bother you, but I'm hoping you'll be able to do me a favor. I'm trying to write a book about heroes in my life and how they have made America a better place. I think it might be interesting to people because I'm still a kid.

I already have Pete Seeger's permission to interview him (that was kind of easy because he came to Utah and performed with Children's Dance Theater last year, and I danced with that company, so we got to know each other a little bit). I like that he has spent his life trying to make things better for minorities and working-class people.

Now I'm hoping that my other heroes will also agree to let me talk with them. It will be hard, I think, because the reason I admire them is that they are changing the world, in little ways. But I bet that that keeps them pretty busy.

Dad and I plan to drive to New York sometime this spring. My sister might come because she's looking at colleges she might go to. My mom has six kids, so she is too busy to come. I will interview Pete Seeger, and my dad will take some photos (he once was a professional photographer). I would really like to be able to meet with you while I'm there. I'd come to wherever you are, and I'd have read everything about you that I can find in the library and have written down questions so that I wouldn't have to waste too much of your time.

I know that people would rather read your books themselves than read about you in my book, but I still think it would be very interesting. Please think about it. I promise that I'll be just as little trouble as possible.

Thanks a lot, and please keep writing!

Sincerely,

William Hatch

"*I think we're all heroes if you catch us at the right moment. We all have something noble and decent in us trying to get out. And we're all less than heroic at other times.*

"*It's the media that notices one person at one moment and not another. I'm just like the next person—full of frailty, with some courage, some decency, mixed in.*

"*You think I'm a hero. To me a hero is just a symbol of what's good in all of us. You're looking at me, and maybe you just notice what's good in yourself.*"

—Andy Garcia as John Bubber in *Hero*

1

Pete Seeger

At age eighty-five, Pete Seeger has many accomplishments to look back on. During his life he has been a songwriter, writing songs such as "If I Had a Hammer," "We Shall Overcome," and "Turn! Turn! Turn!" He has been a singer, who some people believe helped start the widespread interest in American folk music that led to the popularity of musical groups such as Peter, Paul, and Mary and many others. He has made more than a hundred recordings of music and has also been involved with many songbooks, manuals teaching how to play the banjo, and magazine articles. He is famous for his lifelong work as a labor activist and continues to be a persistent voice against war. He is proud of the work he has accomplished as an environmentalist, mainly working to clean up the Hudson River in New York.

In the 1930s, the Great Depression had a devastating effect on the United States. Between 25 percent and 33 percent of the people in this country were out of work, and jobs for them simply didn't exist. Industrial production was down to one-half of what it had been before the Depression, and thousands of people had lost their farms. Many people felt helpless and hopeless. A lot of people lost their faith in capitalism and looked for other economic solutions. There was a great social upheaval in this country, and communism and socialism were solutions that were attractive to a lot of people. Seeger was ten years old when the Great Depression began. His father had been a music professor at the University of California at Berkeley, but his strong antiwar beliefs led to his losing his job. In spite of the fact that both of Seeger's parents were descendents of the original people who sailed on the *Mayflower*, the political attitude in his home as Seeger was growing up was far left.

Pete Seeger was born in a New York City hospital on May 3, 1919. When he was sixteen, Seeger attended a folk song and dance festival and heard the five-string banjo for the first time in his life. He was totally smitten with the instrument and began to be interested in folk music.

After two years at Harvard, where Seeger's political activities got in the way of his studying, he left school and eventually ended up in Washington, D.C., working in the Archives of American Folk Music in the Library of Congress in an entry-level position. During this time he met legendary blues and folk music performers such as Leadbelly, Woody Guthrie, Lee Hays, and the labor militant Aunt Molly Jackson. By the time he was twenty-two he was a skilled musician on the banjo.

In 1941 Woody Guthrie joined Pete Seeger, Lee Hays, and others in forming the Almanac Singers, a group that first recorded labor songs, then pacifist songs. Then in the fall of 1941 they began recording songs supporting the war against Hitler.

When the United States entered the Second World War, the Almanac Singers were suddenly well known throughout the country. They were on national radio broadcasts and sang in some of the fanciest nightclubs in New York City. Seeger joined the army, and he married Toshi Ohta during his first leave. She has played an important role over the past sixty years in managing his career and his finances.

In the forties, Seeger accompanied Henry Wallace, the presidential candidate of the Progressive Party, on a political tour of the South. They regularly had eggs and tomatoes thrown at them, and on September 4, 1949, stones were thrown at the Seegers' car during the infamous Peekskill, New York, riot. His wife and their two young children were in the car with him. Shortly afterward, he and Lee Hays cowrote the song "If I Had a Hammer," which is still sung today and remains popular because of its optimism about social change.

In the early 1950s Seeger formed the singing group the Weavers with Lee Hays, Ronnie Gilbert, and Fred Hellerman. They made a recording of "Goodnight Irene" in June of 1950, which brought them great success. In the meantime, however, the country had been overtaken by a mood of suspicion, blacklisting, and red-baiting. The Weavers' songs fell from where they had been at the top of the charts, and their concert appearances began to be regularly canceled.

In 1953 Pete Seeger starting singing on his own. He still occasionally sang with the Weavers, but he mainly supported his family with appearances at summer camps and colleges, and with the five or six record albums he released each year.

In 1955 the House Un-American Activities Committee subpoenaed Seeger. He is proud that he is one of the very few witnesses called that year who did not invoke the Fifth Amendment to avoid testifying. Seeger said that discussing his political views and his associations would violate his First Amendment rights. It was a very dramatic appearance, and Seeger and seven others, including the playwright Arthur Miller, were indicted for contempt of Congress by an overwhelming majority of the House of Representatives. In 1961 he was found guilty of contempt and sentenced to ten years in prison. The following year, however, the case was dismissed on a technicality.

The folk music revival that Seeger had cultivated in the 1950s gathered momentum in the 1960s, as evidenced by the start of the

Newport Festival. The civil rights movement was making great progress. Seeger visited the South several times during the civil rights marches of the 1960s. His version of an old spiritual became an anthem of the movement. He called it "We Shall Overcome."

Throughout the 1970s and 1980s, Pete Seeger continued to donate his time and his performances to benefit many political causes, but his attention focused more and more on the problems with the environment. With some friends, in 1969 Seeger launched a sloop called the *Clearwater* into the Hudson River. It was a symbolic act, which fulfilled a lifelong love of the outdoors and a deep desire to help clean up the environment, beginning with that river. He has worked on the project ever since then and is proud that the Hudson River has been at least partially cleaned up in the past thirty years.

How Will Got the Interview

My interview with Seeger was the very first one we did. It is also the only interview that took place in the hero's home. All of the rest of them were in their office, a restaurant, or some other public place.

My uncle was getting married in New York, and our family planned to drive there from our home in Idaho, pulling a trailer filled with my uncle's belongings. When we found that the wedding was only thirty miles from where Seeger lives, it seemed too good to be true. Seeger and I had already written to each other a couple of times, so I wrote again and asked if I could meet with him while we were in New York. He agreed.

The day after the wedding, Dad and I left the rest of the family at the hotel and drove up into the foothills. Seeger's home was a comfortable log cabin that he and his wife had built themselves; it had a beautiful view of the Hudson River below.

Interview

THE SEEGER HOME, OVERLOOKING THE HUDSON RIVER,
BEACON, NEW YORK, APRIL 30, 1994

WILL: In your civil rights work you've met people who have become legends, especially Martin Luther King. Did he live up to his legend?

PETE SEEGER: He certainly did. He was a very quiet, thoughtful fellow, but when he got started talking he made so much sense that all sorts of people listened to him—white people as well as black people, and old people as well as young people. He was, really, one of the most extraordinary speakers I'll ever hear in my life. That doesn't mean he was perfect. He was human and made mistakes like any other person. You've heard of the statement, "All idols have feet of clay." I make mistakes, and I hope you don't try to make—I hope nobody tries to make a hero out of me.

Actually, if there's any hero in my family, it's the woman you met, my wife, who kept this family together when I was traveling all over the world. And it was not easy. In the wintertime she had to plow the snow. And sometimes she'd be at home with two little babies and hear the dog bark-bark-barking, and wondering if there's some man out there going to try and do something. But she was very, very brave. And whenever I think of heroes I think of people like her because a lot of women have been absolutely heroic in raising children when the man was not there when he should have been. And I'd come home after a while, but it wasn't good that I was away from home so much.

WILL: What was Martin Luther King like?

PETE SEEGER: Martin Luther King, as I said, was very quiet. He could joke at times, but he was essentially a rather serious person. He had a rather quiet sense of humor. I didn't know him well. I met him on a few occasions where he was speaking and I was singing. But those were heroic times, and what he did was bring out the heroism in a whole lot of other people. And I tried to tell people about it through song.

Like the children of Birmingham in 1963. They had demonstrations, and some were thrown in jail. Well, Dr. King at one time said something like, "Young people, we've got to have a silent demonstration. We've got to show that we are disciplined, and so we're going to walk down the street silently. No shouting, no talking, no singing." And they all left the church determined to do what he said. No one was speaking.

Before they left, someone raised his hand. "Dr. King, what if we're arrested?" "Oh," he says, "if you're arrested then do whatever you want, after that."

Well, they walked down the street just as dignified and quiet. People were shouting insults at them from the sidewalk, but they didn't reply. But down the road came a batch of policemen on motorcycles. They pulled right in front of them and shouted, "You're all under arrest."

Well, it could have been rehearsed. They might have been practicing a dance. They had a special dance step and a song. "Ain't a-scared of your jail 'cause I want my freedom. I want my freedom. I want my freedom. Ain't a-scared of your jail 'cause I want my freedom. I want my freedom now."

There were a couple of other verses. "Ain't a-scared of your dogs 'cause I want my freedom." You know, the policemen were calling out big dogs to bite the little kids, and they had a hose, they were hosing them down. "Ain't a-scared of your hose, 'cause I want my freedom." And they were dancing to it as they took them off to jail.

WILL: Were you ever in jail during that time?

PETE SEEGER: Not during that time. I've been in jail at other times, not for very long periods of time. I was never mistreated. I was never beaten in jail. Some of those people were beaten while they were in jail, and some of them were almost killed.

WILL: Were you ever afraid that people were going to physically hurt you?

PETE SEEGER: Oh, there were times. Once there was a whole mob of people that tried to throw stones. They did throw stones at me and a whole batch of others in a little town near here called Peekskill. It's on the Hudson River.

A great black singer named Paul Robeson, he's dead now, but he was one of the greatest men, one of the greatest singers I ever knew. He was giving a concert, and he asked me if I would sing a few songs at the beginning. It was an outdoor concert, and like ten thousand people came. It was a big crowd. We didn't know, but the Ku Klux Klan hated Robeson so much, they were determined they were going to hurt him and anybody else. When the crowd left the concert field, there were some policemen directing traffic. I wanted to turn left because I lived up here. "No. All cars go down this way." All the cars had to go down one street.

The police knew what was going to happen. There was a police conspiracy, I think. We hadn't gone more than one hundred feet and I saw some glass in the road and I said to my family, "Oh-oh. Be prepared to duck. Somebody may throw a stone." Well, that was the understatement of the year. Around the corner was a young man with a pile of stones about waist high, each stone about as big as a baseball. And every car that came by, *Wham!*—with all his strength he threw a stone at the window.

Well, every window in our car was broken, and at least two stones came through and landed on the floor. Everybody but me had put their heads way, way down. So they got glass in their hair and in their clothes, but no one was hurt. One man in one of the other cars lost his eyesight. But being tall (I was driving) I stuck my head up as high as I could, glass is flying all around here, but I kept on driving.

Well, at the next corner there was another man with a pile of stones. And around the next corner there was another man with a pile of stones. On both sides of the road were young people with piles of stones, and there was a policeman standing right there, about sixty feet away from a man throwing stones. And I stopped the car. I tried to roll down the window. I couldn't roll it very far down because the glass was splintered. I said, "Officer! Aren't you going to do something?" He just shouted, "Move on. Move on."

I looked around. Because I had stopped, the car in back of me had stopped. And he was getting stone after stone. He was going to get killed. So I moved on. About five years ago I was singing in Denver, Colorado, and a man my age came backstage after the concert, along with some younger people. He says, "Pete, you were at Peekskill weren't you?" "Yeah." "I was in the car behind you." "Well," I said, "I bet you were glad when I moved on!" He said, "Yeah. I sure was."

Well, I found out later the Ku Klux Klan had organized that whole thing. I don't know if you know about the Ku Klux Klan?

WILL: Yeah.

PETE SEEGER: They had members in the police department. I found out from a young man who lived in Peekskill. I said, "How did you find out about this?" He said, "Oh, my father was in the police force. I was just a kid at the time." But he said, "Pete, they had that whole concert area surrounded with walkie-talkies like a battlefield. You guys didn't have a chance."

Well, nobody was killed, I'm glad to say. But ten thousand people had stones thrown at them. Some people thought this was going to be the beginning of a dictatorship here, of Fascism taking over America.

WILL: Did you feel noble, or just angry?

PETE SEEGER: Oh, I was concerned. Funny, I didn't really feel angry so much as very concerned.

Once a headline in the newspaper said, "Pete Seeger sings anti-American song in Moscow." Wow. This was in 1967. Some people went down Main Street with a petition to sign that I should not be allowed to sing in the high school. Our doctor, who was a liberal man, said, "Pete, you ought to cancel this concert at the high school. You're going to be run out of town. This is Fascism. You know it."

But my wife and I decided it was worth making a stand. And sure enough, some of the kids stuck up for us, and finally some of the respectable people stuck up for us.

I had not sung an anti-American song in Moscow. It was a rather sad song about a guy killed in Vietnam, but it wasn't anti-American in any way. It was a true story. I took the words out of a local newspaper. A woman right across the river said, "My husband's dead now. But this is what he wrote me last month: 'We've got no friends here. It's my own troops I have to watch out for.'" He was an American adviser with Vietnamese troops. He said, "I sleep with a pistol under my head."

So I turned it into rhyme. "It's my own troops I have to watch out for, he said. I sleep with a pistol right under my head. He wrote this last month. Last week he was dead. And Simon came home in a casket."

Well, in 1967, one Sunday the woods caught fire up here, about a hundred yards away. I was a member of the local volunteer fire department, and we came and put it out. The next Sunday the woods caught fire down here about two hundred yards away. Again it was put out. Well, some of my neighbors knew who had set it. And they said to him, "You trying to burn the mountain down just because you don't like Seeger?" And that was the last he tried it.

WILL: I noticed in your book *Where Have All the Flowers Gone* that you worked really hard to make sure that the right people get the royalties for the songs you perform. And you've given away the profit for a lot of your more popular songs, like "We Shall Overcome," "Wimoweh," and the profits from the book itself. Since you're so generous with your profits, how do you support yourself and your family?

PETE SEEGER: Thanks to the world copyright law, when one of my songs is played on the radio I get a fraction of a penny. Just a fraction of a penny. But you know, it all adds up. The song "If I Had a Hammer" has been played millions of times on the radio. Let's see; if I got one penny from that, wow. That would be like twenty thousand dollars for each million plays. Just from that one song.

And living up here on the mountain we don't have to pay rent. We pay a few thousand dollars in taxes, but that's not as much as rent would be. And we eat mostly food out of the garden. And we don't buy fancy clothes and go to fancy shows. We do have two cars. They're our big expense. One, because sometimes I'm traveling away using one car and my wife, Toshi, needs another car here. The other car is like a truck. We can haul a trailer, like your car does, haul logs and stones.

WILL: I'm from Utah, which is a conservative state. My grandpa is one year younger than you. He's very active in the Republican Party and has held state office and still believes that Richard Nixon was innocent. It's hard for me to picture someone my grandpa's age who has belonged to the Communist Party for fifty years, like you have.

PETE SEEGER: No, I was a member for about thirteen years. I dropped out around the early fifties. On the other hand, it depends how you define Communism. At the end of my book, I say that I guess I'm still a Communist. I'd like to see a world without millionaires. So I do disagree with your grandfather pretty strongly in some ways. But I think you'd be surprised. I probably agree with him in other ways.

WILL: Your book says you didn't smoke, drink, or chase girls. So that part was like my grandpa. At what point in your youth did you become radicalized?

PETE SEEGER: Well, I usually make a joke of it, because that's when I first learned about American Indians. There were no rich and poor in an Indian tribe. If somebody shot a deer, there were no iceboxes, so maybe the hunter's wife had the best parts of the deer to cook for supper, but the rest of the deer was shared with the neighbors. No sense in letting the meat go to waste. And so if you study the science of anthropology in college, they'll tell you that the American Indians were "tribal communists." As a matter of fact, whether our ancestors came from Europe or Africa or Asia, at some point our ancestors were also living in tribes and villages where there were no rich and no poor.

Then somebody invented agriculture, and now we have what is called class society. You have a ruling class, and then you have a peasant class that does the work. And you'd have a warrior class, maybe, with the soldiers, and a priest class that made sure that everybody knew the old stories. But a class society came along wherever agriculture came, whether it was in Latin America or in Africa, Asia, or Europe.

With agriculture, people ate better. After all, when you're hunting, there will be some days you'll go without any food, especially in winter. And there's no nuts or berries to eat. A lot of times a hunting society was a society of very thin people! People ate better when we invented agriculture, but you have to take the bad with the good. As I say, agricultural society became class society.

WILL: Why did you become radicalized?

PETE SEEGER: Because of the existence of poverty. It's really unnecessary for anybody to be poor. People say, "Nobody has to be poor if you work hard." But some people work harder than others. And so, of course, they get rich. And then they pass on their riches to their children. After a while the people who have money are not necessarily any more clever or any harder working. In fact, some of the laziest people I've ever known in my life have been some very rich people.

That's really why I became a "radical." Because I don't think it's a sensible way to live to have some people always poor and some people always rich. I really would like to see a world where we can learn to share.

WILL: Have you had opportunities to perform in the Communist bloc?

PETE SEEGER: In 1963, I took my three kids out of school and went around the world. Sang in islands of the Pacific, I sang in Australia, Japan, Indonesia, Africa, India, and sang in Communist Czechoslovakia, and Communist Poland, and Moscow, and Leningrad, it was then. And I could see that it was a very tightly controlled society. I don't think any tightly controlled society will last too long. I really believe that you have to allow people to blow off steam in some way. Or exchange opinions.

In effect, they had a priesthood of Communist Party people who told everybody what they could say and what they couldn't say. That's no way to run a country. I am very glad that the Berlin Wall came down so peacefully. Some people said, "Oh, there's going to have to be a third world war before that wall will ever come down." But they were wrong.

WILL: Were your parents and brothers very politically liberal?

PETE SEEGER: Well, my father was radicalized during World War I. He thought war was a bad thing. His younger brother had enlisted to fight against the Germans. My father wrote him, "Alan, you're a damn fool. Don't you realize that the class of people that run Germany are really not all that different from the class of people that run France? And if you go out to shoot, you're just killing some German working man who's been told he has to go out and join the German army whether he wants to or not. So that's the person you're shooting at."

World War I radicalized my father. He had been the youngest full professor at Berkeley. He set up the music department there at age twenty-five. He was making speeches against imperialist war. And next thing he was fired. My father lost his job as a professor.

Then he came to New York. And when the Crash of 1929 happened, he and his friends said, "Well, this surely is the end of the free-enterprise system. It's either going to be a fascist dictator taking over, or socialism." And he supported the Communists in the twenties. And that's when I got radicalized, too. I joined the Young Communist League while I was in college because they were the ones really out to stop Hitler, Tojo, and Mussolini.

My father dropped out when he read about the Moscow purge trials. Do you know what Stalin did? He had some other people in the leadership who didn't agree with him. And he said, "Oh-oh. If I don't get rid of them they're going to take my job away from me."

He arrested them and tortured them, probably, and got them to confess. When my father read the details, that was the end of it for him.

I stayed on a while. Actually, the Communists I knew, whether they were right or wrong, anybody would agree some of them were very heroic people.

I still sing (in fact I sang Saturday night) "The Ballad of Harry Simms." Harry was a Jewish youth, aged nineteen. He volunteered to be a union organizer down in Kentucky. The organizer up here said, "Harry, it's dangerous down there. You could get shot. People walk around with rifles down there in Kentucky." Harry said, "Well, I'll be careful. But somebody has got to do that job."

And he went down and organized. He was a great speaker, even though he was only nineteen. He said, "We'll never get decent wages unless we join the union."

Walking up the tracks one day, broad daylight, some people paid by the coal company went and shot him in the stomach. And the coal miner who was with him took him to a hospital. But they said, "Oh, we're not sure this man can pay his bill. We can't take him in unless you've got some money."

Harry Simms sat on the curb, holding his bleeding stomach, for two hours. He was bleeding to death. Finally the miner got some people to pledge some money, and they took him in. But he died on the operating table.

So this coal miner, Jim Garland, took an old ballad melody and put words to it. He was a wonderful man. He only died a few years ago. I sang in Portland, Oregon, last week and I sang this song, dedicated not just to Harry Simms, the man who was killed, but also to the man who wrote the song.

And Communists were brave people. They volunteered to fight against Franco in Spain when nobody else was willing to volunteer. They volunteered to fight in World War II. But me? All I did was play the banjo through the war. People who fought in Spain and still lived volunteered to fight against Hitler in World War II.

WILL: How about when you were blacklisted—were your parents and children and wife supportive?

PETE SEEGER: Yes. Of course my children were too young to really know much about it. Probably somebody at school said, "Is your dad a Communist?" and they said, "I dunno. Dad does crazy things—building a log cabin instead of a house like everybody else lives in." But my parents, and my aunt and uncle, and above all my wife and her parents, were supportive.

I was very close to my wife's parents. We lived in the same house in New York when our babies were first born. And when we moved up here they moved up here, too, and got jobs as caretakers of a local children's camp. As a matter of fact, my father-in-law said that the ten years he was caretaker were the happiest ten years of his life—all those kids around. As a Japanese man in this country he always had trouble getting a job. At one time he had a job in the theater and he helped organize the scenery painters' union. And then he couldn't afford to join it! Oh, it was crazy.

And then he was caretaker of this camp—mowing the lawns and putting in the gardens. He was like a grandpa to a lot of those kids. He'd see some kid that was shut out and not getting along, and he'd take him under his wing.

WILL: How did you support your family during those years?

PETE SEEGER: Oh, I sang mostly in schools and camps and colleges.

WILL: When you were blacklisted?

PETE SEEGER: I was blacklisted from the radio, but I didn't expect to make a living in radio anyway. The McCarthy Era was a terrible era for some people. They lost their jobs. They had to move to a different town. But I kept on living in the same house. We had a little children's chorus when we first moved up here. Every Christmas we'd go sing Christmas carols to all the neighbors. But when the House Un-American Activities Committee questioned me, the neighbors got scared and they said, "Better not try and have the chorus." So the chorus disbanded.

But, except for things like that, I didn't have any hardship. We weren't rich. I remember once in the midfifties in San Francisco, I told my friend, "I've got to make at least a hundred dollars a day to make my plane fare and to send some money home to Toshi, my wife." And he wrote back, "Well, I can't get more than twenty-five dollars for you. Are you willing to sing four times a day?" I said,

"Yup." So I'd sing at one school early in the morning for twenty-five dollars, and in the early afternoon another twenty-five dollars, in the late afternoon somewhere else for another twenty-five, and in the evening somewhere else for yet another twenty-five dollars. And I made my hundred dollars.

WILL: In your books you've described how much of your income is given away.

PETE SEEGER: Well, we're very fortunate to be able to give away. Even if I got sick now, Toshi could still pay her bills and the taxes with the royalties coming in. So, I don't give it *all* away.

———————

2

Madeleine L'Engle

Madeleine L'Engle was born Madeleine Camp. She married a well-known Broadway and television actor, Hugh Franklin, and became Madeleine Camp Franklin. She took her writing name from her grandmother's maiden name, which is L'Engle. L'Engle won the Newbery Award for the most distinguished contribution to American literature for children in 1963 for her book *A Wrinkle in Time*. She has also written many other children's novels as well as books of adult fiction. But L'Engle hasn't written only novels; she has published plays, poetry, memoirs, essays, and religious writings. She has published more than sixty books and has won other awards as well as the Newbery.

When L'Engle gave her acceptance speech for winning the Newbery Award she said that very few children have any problems with the world of the imagination. She said that problems are in their own world, the world of their daily life, and as adults it's our loss that so many of us grow out of the world of the imagination. Fortunately for all of us, L'Engle has never grown out of it.

Madeleine L'Engle was born on November 29, 1918, and spent the first twelve years of her life in New York City. Her father was a writer, her mother was a musician, and her parents' home was always filled with artists. Because L'Engle was an only child, she was included in many of the gatherings.

When L'Engle was twelve years old her family moved to the French Alps, and L'Engle attended an English boarding school in Switzerland. It felt like a prison to her, and she was very unhappy there. The students were not called by name but by an assigned number. She was number ninety-seven. The students were also never allowed to be alone, nor to daydream. L'Engle rebelled against the rules by secretly writing stories (which she had been doing since she was five) and by sneaking books to bed with her and reading them under the covers with the help of a flashlight.

One memorable time at the boarding school, L'Engle was in trouble for something she had done and was being reprimanded in front of the other students. Suddenly the teacher decided that L'Engle was also chewing gum and demanded that L'Engle "spit out what is in your mouth into my hand." In fact, L'Engle wasn't chewing gum. However, she took the opportunity to spit into the teacher's hand her dental appliance, which consisted of several false teeth. (She wore it all of the time to replace teeth that had never grown in.) The other students were delighted when the teacher suddenly had a handful of false teeth.

L'Engle returned to the United States to finish high school, and she went to college at Smith, where she studied English and continued with her writing. She enjoyed the time there very much.

After L'Engle graduated with honors from college, she moved to New York City. She had a small apartment in Greenwich Village and worked in the theater. The good pay she earned because she belonged to Equity, the actor's union, combined with the flexible hours of acting left her plenty of time to write. She published her first two novels during this time and also met Hugh Franklin while she was an understudy in the same production of Anton Chekov's play *The Cherry Orchard* on Broadway in which he had a part. They were married a year later.

After their first child was born, L'Engle and her husband moved to Connecticut so that they could raise their family away from the big city of Manhattan. They bought a small general store in a village that had more cows than people in it. Both L'Engle and her husband worked in the store for nine years, while L'Engle continued writing at night. Two more children were born while they were there.

One book that L'Engle wrote during this time was *A Wrinkle in Time*. She had already published six novels and should have had no problem finding a publisher for this one, but no publisher was interested. She spent two and a half years submitting it to twenty-six different publishers, and she was rejected by all of them. This was a very frustrating time for L'Engle. She felt that this was the best book she had yet written, and she was very excited about it, but no publisher would take it. She continued writing, even though none of her other writings were accepted by publishers either.

Finally a friend of hers introduced her to John Farrar, who was a partner in the publishing firm of Farrar, Straus and Giroux, and they bought the manuscript. After it won the Newbery Award many publishers would speak with her and comment that they wished she had brought the manuscript to their publishing company. She told each one that she had brought it to them and had been rejected. One publisher wouldn't believe her until she showed him the rejection slip she had received from his company.

When the Franklin children were ten, seven, and one year old, the family moved back into Manhattan. They moved into a large eight-room apartment overlooking the Hudson River. Franklin began acting again and spent ten years portraying a character named Dr. Charles Tyler on the television series "All My Children." L'Engle began a long association with the Cathedral Church of St. John the Divine. She became the librarian at the Cathedral and still has an office there, more than thirty years later. And L'Engle kept writing.

Hugh Franklin, L'Engle's husband, died in 1986. Since then, L'Engle still divides her time between her same apartment overlooking the Hudson River and their home in Connecticut, which they call Crosswicks.

The family who is at the center of *A Wrinkle in Time* appears in several more of Madeleine L'Engle's books. L'Engle has said that she likes seeing what happens to a character both before and after when they appear in her book. Meg Wallace is the main character in *A Wrinkle in Time*. With her brother and a friend they travel through space and time simultaneously using a shortcut called a "tesseract." L'Engle always researches her books very thoroughly so that the scientific principles are correct.

Meg, her friend, and her brother use love and a refusal to conform as weapons to fight against the evil of total authoritarianism, which has taken over several planets. The idea that you can make a difference in the universe without being an important person is a central theme in *A Wrinkle in Time*. Meg and the other characters are small, young, ordinary people, yet they are called on to do what needs to be done. I think that is a very heroic idea. I think her books are so important because many of them are written for people my age, and their stories revolve around good and evil and give a face to them. Despair is always in the background, waiting to take over the characters' hearts. Her books make the whole struggle of good and evil easier for me to understand.

How Will Got the Interview

Madeleine L'Engle was the second hero I interviewed, after Pete Seeger. For me she is heroic because her whole life has been lived with great moral courage—she has always made her choices based on what her personal beliefs told her was right. And she has left a whole body of wonderful books for both children and adults. Her books not only tell gripping stories but also are full of people my age having to make decisions about basic good and evil.

I wrote lots of letters to L'Engle via her publishers. Then my aunt was on the planning committee for a conference at which L'Engle was to be the guest speaker, and Aunt Peggy got me another address to use. I wrote in care of "general delivery" in the small town in Connecticut where L'Engle has her home, but I never heard back. I really hoped to interview her at the same time that I was in New York to interview Seeger, and that date was coming right up.

I'm not sure if it was me or my mom or dad that had the bright idea of seeing if, by any chance, she was listed in the telephone directory. I looked under her late husband's name, and there she was! I couldn't call her because I was at school during office hours in New York. So my dad agreed to place the call for me.

Dad called the number, and Madeleine L'Engle answered. Dad was so amazed at having actually reached her that his mind went blank. And then he said, "Madeleine? May I call you Madeleine?" which was not at all what he had planned to say. Anyway, he explained the letters and the project. She had never received any of the letters but kindly agreed to meet with me while we were in New York. My dad would accompany me to take photographs.

We met L'Engle in the library of St. John's Episcopal Cathedral in New York City. It is a beautiful and huge building with a sculpture garden and other gardens surrounding it. Her office was in the cathedral library. I remember thinking how comfortable and cozy it felt. I also remember that there were books everywhere and stacks on every available surface. It seemed almost scholarly—much as I would imagine the study of Gandhi, Einstein, or one of the other great thinkers would have been. It was dusty and a little untidy—a wonderful place to write stories.

When we got to her office she was very polite and attentive. We talked for a while—she at her desk and I in a chair across from her. I remember feeling that her eyes were like an owl's—very wise and looking as if she saw more than other people do.

After we had chatted for a minute, L'Engle and my dad and I went out to a small Italian restaurant (one of her favorites) just across Amsterdam Avenue from the cathedral. Her leg was sore, and we walked very slowly to the restaurant. It was very cool for me to sit and chat and have lunch with this woman who had written such original and thought-provoking work.

After lunch we walked back to the cathedral library for the formal interview. There was little to no hesitation in her answers. She talked with the confidence of a professor. I remember being very impressed at the quiet office she had made for herself in the library.

Interview

ST. JOHN'S EPISCOPAL CATHEDRAL, NEW YORK CITY, MAY 4, 1994

WILL: Where do you like to go to write, or is it just wherever you happen to be?

MADELEINE L'ENGLE: Anywhere I'm not interrupted. It doesn't matter where.

WILL: Do you prefer inside or outside?

MADELEINE L'ENGLE: I write anywhere I can. I think solitude is essential for the development of the human psyche, and I've learned to put a force field of silence around me. And within that force field I can go on writing my stories and poems and dreaming my dreams. And that has been very important to me—because I can write anywhere. As long as I'm not responsible for whatever is causing the noise, I can write anywhere, wherever I am. Once I learned to let the pilot do the flying, I can write on planes, or in hotels. The only time my force field has failed me is when I had crawling babies.

WILL: When you sit down to write, how many hours at a time do you like to spend?

MADELEINE L'ENGLE: Ideally, about five. And the rest of the time I'm doing research. But I like to have five hours at a stretch to write. When I'm working on a book I focus on it completely. And I'm apt to go right off into the story while I'm cooking dinner. The dinner doesn't suffer, but if someone is talking to me, I'm not really there. I'm in the story.

WILL: Do you use a word processor?

MADELEINE L'ENGLE: It all depends. I used a manual typewriter, then an electric typewriter. There's not that much difference.

WILL: How long does it generally take you to write a book?

MADELEINE L'ENGLE: About eighteen months. Sometimes a little more, sometimes a little less. It's work. It's a full-time job.

WILL: Is that how long your first book took?

MADELEINE L'ENGLE: Yes. I wrote about half of my first book in college. I came back to New York, sent out the stories I'd written in college to various literary magazines, and got letters from editors asking if I was writing a novel—which of course I was. And I gave the book to the first editor who wrote me. They optioned it for one hundred dollars—which even back then was not much money for someone—and I wrote it.

I happened to get a very good editor who helped me to see what I needed to do to take this shapeless, bulky material and shape it into a book.

WILL: Do you always know ahead of time what's going to happen in the story?

MADELEINE L'ENGLE: Not always. When I wrote the book *The Arm of the Starfish*, the character Joshua just showed up. I didn't plan for him to be part of the book. When I finished the final draft I read it out loud to my mother and my then ten-year-old son. When I got to the scene where Joshua is shot and killed, my son said, "Change it."

"I can't change it," I said. "That's what happened."

He said, "You're the writer. You can change it."

"I can't change it. That's what happened."

I didn't want Joshua to die, either. But that's what happened. If I tried to change it, I'd be deviating from the truth of the story.

WILL: I'd like to talk to you for a moment about when you were my age.

MADELEINE L'ENGLE: How old are you?

WILL: I'm eleven. I know that your childhood was pretty lonely. You felt shy, gawky, and clumsy and sought refuge in books. Plus you only ate one meal a week with your parents—Sunday lunch—and the rest of the time you were just with a nanny.

MADELEINE L'ENGLE: Uh-huh. It was very unsuccessful. My childhood was not very much fun. I was living in New York. My father was dying. I was an only child. I was lame. There were some nice things. But it wasn't a nice, normal, fun childhood. I've had a lot of fun since—I've made up for it.

WILL: In *A Wrinkle in Time*, when you describe the Murray family with the mom's laboratory just off the kitchen, or in *Meet the Austins*, when you describe the Austin family, are you really describing what you wish your childhood had been like?

MADELEINE L'ENGLE: Well, I suppose with the Austin family I was describing what I hoped my family *was* like. And the Murray family, too, is more of my own family than my childhood family. I mean, I was at the typewriter, not at the Bunsen burner, but I did manage to get dinner on. I had my mind on things other than just the kids, but I did manage to keep things going.

WILL: It seems like you didn't even know your parents when you were little, but when you were an adult you were very close to them. Weren't you mad at them for sending you to awful schools and making your childhood so lonely?

MADELEINE L'ENGLE: Well, children seem to take what happens as what happens. And we don't tend to get mad at them. I read a book by a Frenchman who said for a child what happens is from God, and is good. So I just took it for granted. I didn't like it. But I had enough intuitive sense to know that this was not necessarily my parents' choice. It was forced on them because my father had been gassed in the First World War, and they were trying to take care of him.

WILL: How could you end up so close to them?

MADELEINE L'ENGLE: They were nice people. And when I got old enough so that I wasn't their problem, but could live my own life, I had a chance to learn who my mother was and what she was like. I didn't really with my father, because he died when I was seventeen.

WILL: What kind of music did you like when you were my age?

MADELEINE L'ENGLE: I liked the popular music of the day, which was really at that point very pretty. It was very melodic, very different from your rock. But I also loved Bach and Mozart and Handel, and the classical musicians.

WILL: Did you ever have a pet?

MADELEINE L'ENGLE: A pet? Well, after we were in New York I was given a funny little more-or-less-Maltese poodle, and one of my father's friends called him Milk of Magnesia. And his name was Maggie. When we left, we left Maggie, and I missed Maggie.

I didn't have a pet again until I got out of college and was working in the theater and I was in a play called *The Cherry Orchard* by Anton Chekhov. There is a dog in that play, and all the actors wanted to have their dogs be in the play, but there's a very loud party scene and all the dogs would bark. So they finally had to buy a little French poodle, in the days before they had them distributed into sizes, and they were not yappy. She was wonderful. And I took care of her so there was no question she was my dog.

WILL: Who was your hero when you were my age?

MADELEINE L'ENGLE: My heroes were mostly dead. Other writers. Writers whose works I liked. I liked Madame Curie. I liked the French women painters.

WILL: Would they be pleased with what you have accomplished?

MADELEINE L'ENGLE: I think probably some of them would think, "Oh, well she writes books for kids. She can't be very important." But the best of them would be very pleased.

WILL: For what accomplishment would you like to be remembered one hundred years from now?

MADELEINE L'ENGLE: I would hope I would give people courage to live more openly, and lovingly, and bravely.

WILL: What do you still want to accomplish?

MADELEINE L'ENGLE: Oh, twenty or thirty more books.

WILL: I know that you believe in God; your books are a lot about good and evil. C. S. Lewis said that he wrote his children's books so that when kids had a religious experience they would recognize the feeling. Do you have the same kind of goal?

MADELEINE L'ENGLE: I don't think you have to worry about kids recognizing the feeling. I think that's innate in kids. My goal in writing my books, which are the fantasies which are, I suppose, more of the theological ones, is I'm thinking about things *I'm* interested in. And quite often kids are more willing to be interested than grown-ups are.

I often write them with a young protagonist because I know they're going to be too hard for grown-ups. I don't worry about the kids recognizing. They will.

WILL: How does it make you feel when sometimes parents don't want their kids reading *A Wrinkle in Time* because they think it is anti-Christian?

MADELEINE L'ENGLE: I feel very sad, and I also have a question. When that book was first published, long before you were born, in 1962, it was discovered by the evangelical world as a Christian book. Now not one word of that book has changed. What has changed? Why are people turning on something that they affirmed? And the question is why has so much fear, so much anger, come into the world? *A Wrinkle in Time* is one of the ten most censored books in the United States, along with Mark Twain and *Grapes of Wrath* and *The Diary of Anne Frank*. A lot of my favorite books. What's happened to people? I don't know what's happened to people.

WILL: My sister says that dolphins play an important part in some of your books for teenagers. How did you become interested in dolphins?

MADELEINE L'ENGLE: I've seen dolphins, and it seemed to me that they're way ahead of us on the evolutionary scale. I think they know more about God and more about themselves than we do. So I thought that was fascinating. And I began to study them.

WILL: Have you ever gone swimming with them?

MADELEINE L'ENGLE: Not in one of those dolphin swimming places. In San Diego, where I was for a writer's workshop, I went to the petting pool, and I stayed there all day with one particular dolphin, and then the person who was running this workshop called to see if I could get further into the water with the dolphin. The woman was met with indifference, and "Well, what has she written?" "*A Wrinkle in Time.*" "*A Wrinkle in Time*? That's my favorite book. Bring her over." So I did get in a little deeper with dolphins that way.

WILL: Do you think that they have souls?

MADELEINE L'ENGLE: Yes. Why would any human being have a right to decide who does and who does not have souls? When somebody says to me, "My dog died, and my teacher says he can't go to heaven because he doesn't have a soul," I say, "Well, remember, only the human beings were thrown out of the Garden of Eden. The animals weren't."

WILL: In some of your books the family sings around the dinner table something called the "Tallis Canon." I've never heard it. Could you sing it for me?

MADELEINE L'ENGLE: OK. I had six shots of Novocain yesterday. It got in my voice. I'll do the best I can.

All praise to thee my God this night
For all the blessings of the light.
Keep me, oh keep me, King of Kings
Beneath thy own almighty wings.

It's in the Episcopal hymnal.

WILL: I know that you read a lot when you were a kid. There was one book that you reread at least once a month for two years. Who wrote it?

MADELEINE L'ENGLE: Lucy Maud Montgomery. By far my favorite of hers was *Emily of New Moon*. I also liked E. Nesbit. I liked Jules Verne. I liked George MacDonald. All these books are still available. A lot of them were old when I was a kid, but they have universal qualities.

WILL: I know that your fantasies are based on quantum mechanics and particle physics. You learned a lot about it by reading and asking scientists, even though you have no formal background in physics. Do you think that science and a belief in God are compatible?

MADELEINE L'ENGLE: I think scientists have always felt that it was. It's interesting to me how many of them—not Hawking, but many others—are seeing purpose. Now, whether you want to call purpose God or not is up to you. But if there is a purpose, somebody is behind the purpose. I believe that it is a purposeful universe but not a predetermined universe. That has thrown everything for a loop. Up until Newton everything was predetermined. It was going to happen according to plan. Now, with the fear of chaos, we get a lot more free will. I think that is very exciting. And I don't think it disposes of God at all.

WILL: In your books for young readers, the stories center around three families, the Murray family (in the Time trilogy), the Austins, and the O'Keefes. Will they all ever be in the same book?

MADELEINE L'ENGLE: I don't think so. Just friends in common. I think I'm going to keep them apart.

WILL: As I read about you, you reminded me a lot of your character Meg in *A Wrinkle in Time*. Her teachers thought she was stupid in school. She had to learn to have faith in herself, and to do things for herself, whether she was scared or not. Is that right?

MADELEINE L'ENGLE: Well, anything anyone writes is autobiographical. The main thing is my teachers thought I was stupid. There was no point doing work for them, so I didn't do any work, and [I] went home and wrote stories. I didn't learn a thing in school until I got into high school, where I had wonderful teachers. And college. The other years—other than [when] I worked and read at home—were a waste.

WILL: I got confused. Would you just straighten out for me your dad's name—is it Charles Camp or Wallace Franklin? I know that Charles Wallace Murray is a central character in the Time trilogy, and you called him after your father, but I can't figure out exactly what your dad's name was.

MADELEINE L'ENGLE: Charles Camp is my father. Wallace Franklin is my father-in-law. Very wonderful men.

WILL: Are you sorry for the hard times you had as a child?

MADELEINE L'ENGLE: Good question. I began writing every day after school when I was in the fourth grade. I was lame. I was no good in sports. I was always the last chosen for teams, and my side always lost. The teacher thought that if I wasn't good at sports I obviously wasn't very bright either. So I learned there was no point doing homework for her—she'd only put it down in some way.

I'd go home and dump down my books—which I wouldn't look at—and I'd go into the real world where I wrote stories, played the piano, read books, dreamed dreams. It was much too interior a life. But I developed a discipline for writing, which I never would have done if I'd been a successful child at school, playing with my peers.

As I look back on my childhood—and most of my life—it is very apparent to me that the things that would seem to be the most negative were the most important in forming me as a writer, and a woman, and a human being.

3

Florence Griffith-Joyner

Florence Griffith-Joyner was known as the "World's Fastest Woman." She won three gold medals at the 1988 Seoul, Korea, Summer Olympics, and two of the world records she set have still not been equaled. Her beauty and her astonishing speed combined to make women's track a much more popular spectator sport.

Flo Jo (her nickname after the 1984 Olympics) was born December 21, 1959, in California. Her name was Delorez Florence, but her family called her Dee-Dee. She spent her childhood in the projects of south central Los Angeles.

"The projects" is a name for low-income or rent-subsidized housing in large cities. They are usually large groups of huge apartment buildings with little or no landscaping or public areas. Most of the apartments were built many years ago, so they are often small and not well maintained. Public housing was often built in very poor neighborhoods.

Griffith-Joyner was the seventh of eleven children in her family, and her parents divorced while she was still quite young. Her mother taught the values of individualism and independence to her children from a young age. She was a strict parent and didn't allow television during the week.

When Flo Jo was seven years old she began running at the Sugar Ray Robinson Youth Foundation. In 1965 she won the Jesse Owens National Youth Games. By the time she was in high school she was a star athlete and also a straight-A student. She had a strong, unquenchable determination to succeed.

In 1980 Griffith-Joyner tried out for the Olympic team but didn't qualify. But in 1982 she won a National Collegiate Athletic Association championship by running 200 meters in 22.39 seconds. The next year she won another NCAA championship by running 400 meters in 50.94 seconds.

Although she had to drop out of college for a time to help out financially at home, Flo Jo graduated from the University of California at Los Angeles in 1983 with a degree in psychology. Griffith-Joyner won a silver medal at the 1984 Olympics. A couple of quiet years followed. She worked as a bank secretary and built a business based on her hair-braiding skills. Each style would take from four to thirteen hours for her to create and had many tiny individual braids but would last for many weeks.

On October 10, 1987, in Las Vegas, Nevada, she married her track coach, Al Joyner, who is also an Olympic gold medalist. In the 1984 Los Angeles Summer Olympics, Joyner became the first American in eighty years to win a gold medal in the triple jump. He jumped fifty-six feet seven and a half inches.

At the 1988 Olympic trials in Indianapolis, during the quarter-finals Flo Jo set the 100-meter record of 10.49 seconds. Since then no one else has even broken 10.60. When she was at the Seoul Olympics that year she ran a 10.54 and won the gold medal.

She also won the gold medal that year for the 200-meter dash, and that world record also still stands. She actually broke the world record in the semifinals, and then broke her own record in the finals, by running 200 meters in 21.34 seconds.

Her third gold medal was in the 400-meter relay. She also won a silver medal when the U.S. team, with Flo Jo as the anchor, ran the 1,600-meter relay. Later that year she was voted the U.S. Olympic Committee and Associated Press Female Athlete of the Year, and she won the Sullivan Award as the nation's top amateur athlete. She was also given the Jesse Owens Award as an outstanding field and track athlete.

Not only could Flo Jo run as fast as most male runners, she had other remarkable talents as well. She was a wonderful fashion designer. She designed her own running outfits, which were always bright and often glittery. They were daring and unusual, sometimes covering just one shoulder. At the Seoul Olympics, one of her running outfits was a purple bodysuit with a turquoise bikini brief over it that left one leg bare. She called this kind of design a "one-legger." In 1989 she helped design new uniforms for the Indiana Pacers basketball team.

Griffith-Joyner wore her fingernails very long—sometimes even six inches long. She would paint them with elaborate designs. At the Seoul Olympics she painted three of her fingernails red, white, and blue, and she painted a fourth fingernail gold. She said that the gold was to suggest her goal of winning the gold medal. She wore her long hair loose when she ran, and it would flow behind her making a very exotic image.

In 1989 Flo Jo became the spokeswoman for the American Cancer Society, the Multiple Sclerosis Foundation, and Project Eco-School. The next year the Joyners had a daughter, Mary Ruth.

After the Seoul Olympics, Flo Jo became involved in sportscasting, writing, and directing and also concentrated on being a mother. She was proud of her appointment as cochair of the President's Council on Physical Fitness and Sports and worked hard in that capacity. In 1994 the Joyners started the Florence Griffith-Joyner

Foundation for disadvantaged youth. The next year she was inducted into the U.S. Track and Field Hall of Fame.

Florence Griffith-Joyner died unexpectedly on September 21, 1998, in Mission Viejo, California, where she and her family were living. She was only thirty-eight years old.

For me Flo Jo is a hero not only because she was the fastest woman in the world. I like that she had many sides to her. She seemed shy, but she did what she wanted to do and was able to ignore ridicule. She persevered in her running, even when she was in pain. She had wonderful dreams and goals for herself, and she just kept going until she accomplished them. She was not immune to defeat, or heavy odds, but she was determined to win. And she was such a lovely, gracious, kind person while she did it.

How Will Got the Interview

It took a while to get in touch with Griffith-Joyner. I wrote to managers, friends, and publicists. My dad gave me contact information with many sports journalists who had covered her. At the time of our interview, in 1996, she was at the peak of her career, very busy, and very active in her daughter's life and in programs for other children.

We were planning on going to Southern California, but we still hadn't connected with Griffith-Joyner, and I was feeling desperate because I wanted to interview her on the trip. The day before we left for California my dad and I spent a couple of hours calling everyone we could think of who might possibly have a connection to her. Finally, someone at *Sports Illustrated* magazine gave us a phone number for her foundation, and she answered the phone herself! I immediately sent her a letter, by fax, that explained my project, and she agreed to meet me a couple of days later.

She was the most supportive of all the heroes I talked to. One thing that still stands out is how disciplined she was both physically and mentally. She gave her full and undivided attention to each question and was very polite and to the point. She was also really nice about taking all the pictures.

Another thing that struck me was her dedication to her daughter. At one point I asked her if she planned on getting her daughter into running, and she replied that she would support her in whatever she did but would not force her into anything. On that same note, she talked about how poor she had been growing up. She didn't talk about it with shame or regret but as if she saw it as an opportunity, a challenge, and an environment that provoked growth. She laughed as she told me about hand-me-downs and broken toys. She spoke fondly of taking care of brothers and sisters. Those things definitely show in the person she became.

Another thing I thought was cool was the fact that Flo Jo practiced running at a high school track (where we met her for the interview). If I hadn't seen her pictures on TV, I would have thought she was just another jogger. I guess I had always envisioned Olympic runners sweating and bleeding and grunting with exertion, but she wasn't. Flo Jo was a person who loved what she did, and it showed in her beaming smile that's visible in almost all her race pictures. She was a woman who first dreamed things and then made her dreams a reality.

I think that Florence Griffith-Joyner is a hero not only because she is the fastest woman in the world but also for other significant reasons. She seemed like a paradox. She was shy, but she did what she wanted to do and was bravely immune to ridicule. Because she was encouraged in all her interests by her mother, Griffith-Joyner grew up a natural eccentric, different not for the sake of being different but for the sake of being herself.

I had the interview with Griffith-Joyner on June 4, 1996. I didn't transcribe the interview until after she had died. It made me feel very sad to hear her voice on the tape, talking about all her plans, because I knew that she had not lived long enough to make them happen. She talked about how painful it is to train in track for many hours every day and that she's thinking about doing acting instead. It made me realize how much she had sacrificed to make her running dreams a reality. I even wonder if she just wore her heart out in half the usual years because she pushed herself so hard physically.

◆

Interview

Will: I'd like to talk to you for a minute about when you were my age. Who were your heroes back then?

Florence Griffith-Joyner: Wilma Rudolph was my inspiration as far as athletes were concerned. Muhammad Ali. But my parents were my role models back then, and they still are, because I looked up to them. They were very positive. They still are. And they taught me to believe in myself, no matter what it was in life that I wanted to become.

Will: Are they still your heroes?

Florence Griffith-Joyner: Yes. Unfortunately Wilma Rudolph passed away last year, but her inspiration still lives within me, because it's her accomplishments that I tried to emulate. She went to the 1960 Olympic Games and won three gold medals. I went to the 1988 Olympic Games and won three gold medals and one silver. So I always tell people, "Well, I surpassed Wilma by one medal." But she was a great inspiration in my life—not only because of her athletic accomplishments but as a person as well. And she was one of twenty-two kids. And I am one of eleven—half the amount. So I kind of tell myself that I was similar to her.

Will: I know you started running when you were seven. How did you happen to start?

Florence Griffith-Joyner: I ran in elementary school, and then I joined the Sugar Ray Robinson Youth Foundation, and through his organization I competed in track and field, swimming, basketball, potato sack races, and every Saturday we went to the park and we just had fun, ran, and played a lot of games. But it was through the Sugar Ray Robinson Youth Foundation that I began my athletic career. And I've been running ever since.

WILL: Did you love it from the beginning?

FLORENCE GRIFFITH-JOYNER: Yes. I loved running from the very beginning because I felt free when I ran. I felt like nothing else mattered to me when I ran back then, when I first started. Nor does it matter to me when I run today, because I get so much excitement and so much joy out of running.

That's why I do it, because I just love the sport so unconditionally. I don't look at "what happens if I lose?" "What if I win?" To me as long as I get out there, I do the best job that I'm capable of doing. I've trained hard for it. I believe in myself, that I will accomplish my goals. I don't worry about what place I take. As long as I do my best, I'm a winner within myself each time.

WILL: When did you first know that you wanted to spend the rest of your life running?

FLORENCE GRIFFITH-JOYNER: Before I actually started competing in track and field we used to race in the neighborhood where I grew up in south central Los Angeles. I said, "Wow. Wouldn't that be nice for me to be able to feel this good about something I love so much for the rest of my life?" So I chose, at a very early age, to continue running throughout my entire life. And again, it's so important that whatever you do in life, that you enjoy it. I'm so happy that I found a sport that I love so much and receive so much excitement out of that I want to do it for the rest of my life.

WILL: By the time you were my age your parents were separated. How did your mom support you and all your siblings?

FLORENCE GRIFFITH-JOYNER: It was very difficult for my mom to raise all of us with my father being away and them being divorced. It was hard because as kids you want both your parents to stay together forever, and you want to be able to go to your dad whenever you want to talk to him. You want to be able to go to your mom whenever you want to talk to her.

For me, I just had to accept it. But I always believed that one day they would get back together. And I never ever lost faith that they would. But they didn't. It's just that holding on to that little piece of hope helped me to get over a lot of things. I would cry at night and just pray that they would get back together. But they didn't.

But my mom did a great, great job raising all of us on her own once they were divorced. And my father still supported us once they were divorced. I just wish, as a child, that we could have seen him a lot more. We only saw him on vacations, like at Christmas or Easter, or he came down on his own. But it wasn't like seeing my mom every single day. It's like sometimes I just wanted to say, "Hey, Dad, Daddy, can I talk to you?" And he wasn't there. I would always have to write a letter. And that hurt me as a child. But like all things, I got over it. I was able to just accept that my parents weren't going to get back together.

WILL: Did you have a pet when you were a child?

FLORENCE GRIFFITH-JOYNER: Yes, when I was a child we had several dogs. No cats. As I got older, in junior high school, I wanted a snake so bad, but my mom kept saying, "No snakes! No snakes!" So, eventually, when I got to high school, she allowed me to get a snake. And not only did I go and get one snake, I got three snakes! My mother nearly had a fit. But she accepted it and got used to them. As long as I made sure that I fed them and the cages were securely locked on the aquarium she had no problem.

But, I tell you, the first day she was like hysterical. "Get it out! Get it out! Get away! No snakes in this house!" But she always knew that I had a unique style about everything. Call me different, or whatever. Everybody thought I was crazy when I told them I wanted a snake. They didn't believe it until I actually saved up my money and went and bought these three snakes. It took a while for everybody to get used to it. But eventually they did.

WILL: What music did you like?

FLORENCE GRIFFITH-JOYNER: Gospel music has always been my favorite because I was raised as a Christian, and my mom took us to church. I got so attached to Christian music that that's where my love for music is. But I listen to all types of music. I listen to rhythm and blues. I listen to rap. I listen to jazz. I listen to country. I love classical. I love the blues. Because I'm in so many different feelings all the time, if I feel a little bit of country today, I want to hear a little bit of country music. But every day I listen to gospel music, because it is my favorite.

WILL: Did you like to read?

FLORENCE GRIFFITH-JOYNER: Yes, I loved to read. When I was little I thought that would be the last thing that I would want to do when I would grow up, because my mom made us get a book every time we told her, "Mom, we're bored, can we go outside?" She would say, "No. You're not going outside. Go find a book and read it." And we read every book in the house. I remember she bought a whole set of encyclopedias. And when we ran out of the fun books (because we didn't think the encyclopedias were fun) she would pick a subject for us to go and look in the encyclopedia and do a report on that.

So I vowed, "When I grow up I'm not going to read any books!" But it was just to be contrary. When I grew up I read almost every book I could get my hands on. And I still do read a lot. I read to my daughter and she reads to herself. Reading is just a part of my family, and I'm glad that my mom made me do that, and made all of my sisters and brothers, because we enjoy and understand the importance of reading at a young age.

WILL: What were your life goals when you were my age?

FLORENCE GRIFFITH-JOYNER: I knew I wanted to go to the Olympic Games. That was my goal as far as an athlete was concerned. But I wanted to be a seamstress, a designer, an artist, and an actress as well.

Watching movies like *The Wizard of Oz*, which is my favorite movie of all time, I wanted to be like Judy Garland. I wanted to be on the big screen. And I still do. That's a goal of mine. I've done a television movie over in Japan, entitled *The Chaser*. And I had a lot of fun doing it. I would like to work more with an acting coach, as

I did for the movie in Japan, because I got a lot of enjoyment out of it. So that's another one of my dreams that I'm going to pursue a lot more after this year.

I've always wanted to be a writer. I've written thirty-three children's books. I'm working on an autobiography. I haven't been published yet. Publishing companies are looking at them now, so I'm just keeping my fingers crossed and hoping that someday they'll be published.

I started writing children's books because I have thirty-three nieces and nephews, and when they used to come over and spend the night they always wanted me to tell them a story. So I would tell them a story. And then the next night when they wanted me to tell them the story I would forget a part of it, and they'd say, "Well, Auntie Dee-Dee, you forgot this part." And I thought, "OK, well tell me how it went last night." They would tell me and say, "Why don't you just write them down?" And that's how I started writing children's books.

WILL: What more would you like to accomplish?

FLORENCE GRIFFITH-JOYNER: I would like to continue my acting career. When I was dreaming about going to the Olympic Games, the ultimate goal was to be on one of those top podiums, whether it's gold, silver, or bronze. And for me, as an actress, I will work every day, all day if I have to, and I visualize that Oscar being presented to me. So that's one of my ultimate goals.

That would just be, I don't know, it would be like being on top of that podium receiving that gold medal, but a little more, because I don't have to have that physical pain that you get from working out in track and field. You come out here, you train all day, every day. Your body's hurting, your mind is hurting, but you've got to push on because you see yourself get on top of that podium.

For me, as an actress, that physical pain would be eliminated. So I think I would get even more excited knowing I worked really hard, but it wasn't painful.

I would like to see some of my work in museums, some of the artwork that I do. It was such an honor to design for the Discover credit card. And that was a joy because it was something that I love so much, like art. And for someone to say, "We would like for you to design a credit card," that was a great honor for me. I thought, "Wow. I can do a little bit of this, and a little bit of that, and have people say, 'You did a great job.'" That really makes me feel good.

WILL: Do you think that your heroes would be proud of what you've accomplished?

FLORENCE GRIFFITH-JOYNER: I would hope so. I had the opportunity of meeting Wilma Rudolph at the 1988 Olympic Games in Seoul, and we sat for approximately forty or forty-five minutes talking about the differences in time. We compared when she was training, back in the fifties, and competing in the sixties, versus me competing in the eighties. We talked about equipment, the differences in shoes, in tracks, the whole atmosphere of what the Olympic Games were about back then and what they are about today. I'm just so thankful that I had that opportunity to meet her then.

Thereafter we ran into each other a couple of times at the Jesse Owens Awards. So I'm just really blessed that I met her, had the opportunity to talk with her, and to tell her that she had been a great inspiration in my life.

It's like, you want to do the best job you can, for yourself first. Then when you look at those that you call your heroes, like for me Wilma Rudolph and Jesse Owens, and you have the opportunity to meet them, you want them to come to you and say, "You did a great job." And for her to come to me and tell me that I did a great job— well, it just made my life.

WILL: I know that you dropped out of college in 1979 to help support your family. It seems like family must be very important to you.

FLORENCE GRIFFITH-JOYNER: Yes. Family is first in my life. It was a very difficult decision for me to drop out of college at that time. Growing up in poverty, I didn't have the financial support that I would have needed to go to college. I wasn't offered an athletic scholarship. I wasn't offered an academic scholarship. I thought, "How am I going to stay in school?" So I enrolled in school, and I thought, "I really want to run, but I know I have to concentrate on my academics as well." I tried a year of college, and I thought, "I can't continue because I have no financial support." I had to take the bus two hours to school, two hours back. The need was greater than what I could afford.

So I withdrew from school, and I went to work at a bank as a bank teller. And I just saved all my money. While I was working at the bank, my coach at the time, Bob Kersee, came in and he said, "Well, I've spoken with some counselors, and they'd like for you to return to school as much as I would, and they'll help you get financial aid if you'll return." And I thought, "That has to be a promise that I know the money will be there," because I knew that I couldn't afford to stay in school unless I supported myself. So everything was worked out. I went back to school. I got the financial support. I just thank him for coming into my life at the time and making it possible for me to return to school.

The following year he transferred to UCLA and I went to UCLA and finished up three years there.

WILL: I love watching you run—you seem to have such joy. What does it feel like to know that you are the best woman in the world at something?

FLORENCE GRIFFITH-JOYNER: Well, people say I'm the fastest woman in the world; I'm the best in 100 and 200 meters. You think about how many people there are in the world. It's a lot of people. And to say that there's one person that has run faster than any other woman in the world, it's a good feeling—a really good feeling because it tells me that the twenty-some years that I worked following my dreams were worth it. The pain, the agony, the defeat—everything was worth it.

It feels good, but it's hard to really comprehend, because I'm thinking, "Gosh, the world. I mean, what does that really mean—the fastest woman in the world?"

And I know that records are set to be broken, and I know that eventually someone else will come up, because that's what life is all about. So I'm just going to try to hold onto those records, that title, for as long as I can. I just hope that maybe it's my daughter, or a niece, or a friend who will break those records.

What happens when you have a world record or a title like that—the world's fastest woman—it becomes like a best friend to you. So you hold on really tight to it. Eventually that friend leaves you. It feels really good to have such a title, to be considered the best in the world, but you have to feel it in your heart. And, to me, the love I have for my sport makes it all worth it.

I would love to see my daughter run, but I'm not going to push her into it. I know she has an enormous amount of potential at this early age. But she loves gymnastics, and she couldn't care less what Mommy or Daddy does, or Auntie Jackie, because she has her own life. And if she chooses to run we will support her 100 percent. But if she doesn't, we'll go wherever she wants to go.

WILL: Do you think about your title and records every day?

FLORENCE GRIFFITH-JOYNER: No, I don't, because I'm doing so many other things. I don't think about the records and titles every day. I can go a week and not even think about it. It's when I go to the airport, or the grocery store, or come out here to the track and people call, "Flo Jo, may I have your autograph?" Then that reminds me, "OK, I am the world record holder. And I do have a couple of titles." So I just forget about it because I am doing so many other things in my life.

WILL: Could you tell me about your work as cochair of the President's Council on Physical Fitness?

FLORENCE GRIFFITH-JOYNER: Sure. As cochairs of the President's Council on Physical Fitness and Sports, our job is to advise the president on ways that we can improve the health of America, try to get that high cost of health care down, and educate and motivate and try to inspire as many Americans as we can to get fit, get up, and get moving. That's our motto at the council.

We do that through schools. We have a lot of programs. There's the President's Challenge. The President's Fitness Award is where kids try to run as fast as they can, do a mile in ten minutes or less, push-ups, sit-ups, arm reaches, all types of different events to try to receive an award from the president, letting them know that they did a great job.

When I was in junior high school that's what I lived for, to receive that award from the president. They used to give us patches, and I used to sew mine on my gym pants. And every year when they said, "OK, it's time to start training for the President's Challenge," I would work out so hard—push-ups and sit-ups. I received so much joy just getting that patch. My gym teacher brought it to me and said, "Florence, here's your patch." I was like a kid at Christmastime receiving everything I wanted—a kid in a candy store. I just was so happy about receiving it. As cochair, we just try to get those forty million Americans that are living sedentary lifestyles to change, any way we can.

WILL: Do you believe in a God, or that there is a God?

FLORENCE GRIFFITH-JOYNER: Yes, I do believe in God. I was raised as a Christian, and my mom was able to show me the miracles of life through religion. Going to church and experiencing religious miracles (I call them) in my own life has brought my faith to the top where I would never stop believing. I do believe that there is a God, because I know that we've come from somewhere, and we have to go somewhere. And there has to be someone responsible for that. I'm really glad, because I've met so many Christians in my life that have been able to testify that their lives have been able to remain positive with God. And I also have so many family and friends that didn't believe in God, and they have shown me that the negative things that are happening and have happened in their lives are because they didn't believe. And they may have believed more in alcohol, or drugs, or the negative things. So I'm just very thankful that God is a part of my life. He is first in my life and will always be first in my life.

WILL: Where do you keep your gold medals?

FLORENCE GRIFFITH-JOYNER: In a safe-deposit box. We travel around a lot speaking to elementary and junior highs, high schools, colleges, churches. And we take the medals pretty much all the time around with us to show to people.

But when we come back home and we're not going to be on the road for a while we put them in a safety-deposit box. We used to keep them at my home for a long time, but a couple of our friends had their gold medals stolen from their homes. So we thought, "Well, what if somebody breaks in and takes our medals? We'd never get them back!" They don't replace all the medals that are stolen from the athletes. We didn't want to take any chances, so we keep them in the safety-deposit box in the bank.

WILL: Would you tell me about your beautiful long fingernails?

FLORENCE GRIFFITH-JOYNER: Well, when I was in elementary school I became really fascinated with how some people could grow long fingernails and some couldn't. And I was one of those people that couldn't grow them long.

I had one sister whose fingernails grew about two and a half inches and I just thought, "I know there has to be a way I can grow my fingernails long." The first thing she told me was to stop biting my nails. I tried that and it helped a little bit.

But it wasn't until I was in junior high school in my sewing class that they got really long. I would take chalk, like chalk that you write with on the blackboard, and put it underneath my nails to have like a French manicure look. And everybody complimented me on my nails. They'd say, "Well, Florence, they're growing so long." So I thought, "That's it! That's what I will continue to do."

Eventually this one index fingernail grew to be two inches when I was in high school. People just couldn't believe it. So I discovered how I could grow long nails. And my next goal was to see how long they would actually grow. So I let my left hand get six and a half inches! After that I thought, "OK, I know what to do to make it grow." Once I discovered that, that was it.

But I love decorating them. I have my own nail company, FloJo Nails, and we sell nail art. We sell artificial nails as well, but these are my own nails. We sell different colors, we sell glitter, we sell everything you need for fingernails. But I've always loved bright colors, whether they are my fingernails or outfits I design. I just love them. My nails are a reflection of how I feel and who I am.

WILL: Do you design your own running outfits?

FLORENCE GRIFFITH-JOYNER: Sure! I love that, I really do.

I had such a great time designing for the Indiana Pacers when they approached me and asked me to design. I thought, "Sure, I'd love to." And they sent me all the rules and regulations to follow. I thought, "I've never designed for men seven feet tall! I've always designed for women—with pink, lace, something real bright and fancy. When they sent me the regulations, I thought, "Uh-oh. This is something totally different." So I couldn't go way out for the Indiana Pacers.

But I did the best job I could, and I believe I designed around two hundred outfits. And they narrowed it down to that one outfit. And it was by far my favorite. So they're still playing in the outfits that I designed. So that's something else that I really, really love doing—designing. I guess it's all a part of being in the arts.

WILL: You always wear outfits that are really bright or exotic. Is that to "psych out" your competitors, or is that just part of who you are?

FLORENCE GRIFFITH-JOYNER: I wish I could wear outfits that would psych out my opponents! No, I design them with comfort in mind. I design because I love bright colors. I love things that are different.

That came to me as a child because my mom taught me how to sew when I was younger, and I used to sew all my Barbie doll clothes because my mom couldn't afford to buy them. I just loved being able to sew an outfit for Barbie and have a matching outfit for myself, so I was dressed like my Barbie doll. I just got so much pleasure out of that I wanted to continue it for the rest of my life.

Then when my mom would give me something to sew, and I would tell her, "Well, I want to make it like this," she would say, "Well, it's not hard being like everyone else, it's hard being unique. Strive to be different. Everybody can look alike in the same outfit.

Why don't you want something different? Be yourself. You don't have to be like everyone else." And I thought, "Wow. That is right." So, ever since then I've just been designing things that are what people call bizarre or flamboyant. But I love it, and I'm glad she taught me to be myself.

It's not so much being unique; it's being myself. And that was part of who I was back then. I wore my hair different. I wore my clothes different. I'd wear a different sock on each foot every day.

I got teased a lot. Kids really teased me. I don't know if you've ever experienced that. Kids can be really cruel to you. I learned to laugh right along with them because I knew they weren't laughing at me because they didn't know me. They didn't understand me. So what they were laughing at was their inability to accept me.

So I got over it for a while. My mom would say, "Sticks and stones can break your bones, but words can never hurt you." And I'd say, "But Mom, it did hurt when they teased me." And she would say, "I know. It hurts and you want to cry. But you just can't give in to them. You accept yourself and just pray that they will accept you, too." I just learned to laugh right along with them. And today I'm still laughing because they still laugh at what I do. So, you have to learn to accept it.

That's what I try to teach my daughter, Mary. She had a hard time at one point with kids laughing at her for whatever reason—how she pronounced something, I think. So I told her, "Laugh right along with them. Tell them that it's not their fault who you are, but you wish they would accept you. And some kids just don't know better. Some kids you can tell a hundred times not to tease some kids and they never ever learn. You just have to keep explaining it to them."

WILL: If you had to choose one favorite memory from your whole life, what would it be?

FLORENCE GRIFFITH-JOYNER: When my parents were together. I think that was my fondest memory. And I was so young, I just vaguely remember them being together. I don't remember them fussing and fighting. I remember them loving one another. That was just the fondest memory. And in my mind, where I've kept that memory, the happiness is inside my mind as well as my heart. So that's one of the fondest memories I have.

WILL: When I watch you run you look like you are so full of joy and so happy. What do you feel when you watch a tape of yourself running?

FLORENCE GRIFFITH-JOYNER: I feel free when I run; I feel excitement because I'm doing something that I really love. I don't know— it's the only way I can express myself.

It's like when I ran the final on the 100 meters in Seoul in 1988. Twenty meters before I got to the finish line I was so overwhelmed with joy. I knew that I was going to win the gold medal because I didn't see anyone else close by. I thought, "My God! The race is about to be over and I'm going to finally win a gold medal—my first gold medal in the 100 meters." I was never really considered a 100-meter runner; I was always a 200-meter runner. So at the time I was about to prove to myself, and to others, that I was a good 100-meter runner.

So I get so much excitement, joy, and happiness when I run because I'm doing something I really, really love.

WILL: Where does the self-confidence and radiance that you have come from?

FLORENCE GRIFFITH-JOYNER: I believe my self-confidence comes from my faith in God and faith that I have in myself, the belief that my parents instilled in me when I was very young that I could do anything that I wanted to do—anything I set my mind to, and anything that I really believed in.

With each race, no matter how you do, your self-confidence grows because you're telling yourself, "OK, I've accomplished that whether won or lost. I've learned from that. I'm going to move on." So throughout the years of my entire athletic career I have learned from each race, no matter what.

A lot of people say, "Well, what do you learn from winning?" And I'll explain, "You learn how to eliminate the mistakes as best you can. And what I learn from losing is to eliminate the mistakes and try not to make them again." I've won races but still made a lot of mistakes. So each race is different. When you get to the Olympic Games you try to make no mistakes, but again there are always one or two mistakes that your coach will tell you you've made. So I believe my self-confidence has come from every race I've run, every belief I've had in myself, and every dream I've tried to follow, just holding onto it, and never ever letting go of it.

WILL: OK. Do you have any other comments or stories that you'd like to say or tell?

FLORENCE GRIFFITH-JOYNER: I would just like to wish you all the best as you continue your tour and follow your dreams. I was so inspired by your letter that you wrote me about your family, about what you're doing and how wonderful it is to have your dad as your photographer to travel around with you. I just think it's great.

I love to see young people having a dream and just doing the best they can to try to follow it. I just want to say, I wish you all the best. And don't ever let anyone or anything stand in the way, because if it's your dream it's worthwhile working for. It may take a while, because it took me over twenty years to get on that top podium. But because I never ever gave up, and I believed in me and only me, I was able to stand on that top podium and receive a gold medal. So I just want to say thank you for taking the time out to write me, and by all means continue to follow your dreams.

4

Jimmy Carter

Jimmy Carter's mother was a nurse, and so when her baby was ready to be born she went to the hospital in Plains, Georgia, even though her family lived miles away in a very tiny community named Archery, in a time when most people delivered their babies at home. She was proud that she had her baby in the hospital instead of at home. The day was October 1, 1924, and they named their baby James Earl Carter Jr. after his father, who was a businessman and a farmer. James Carter Sr. was strict and inflexible, and he always insisted that Jimmy accomplish the same amount of work in a day as a grown man could, no matter how young Jimmy was. His mother, Lillian Gordy, was a compassionate and generous person who joined the Peace Corps when she was a senior citizen.

Jimmy Carter's parents owned their farmland, but they weren't rich. The home had no electricity for much of his childhood. It was heated with fireplaces. There was no indoor plumbing, so to take a bath they had to haul the water into the house and then heat it on the woodstove in the kitchen.

Carter attended the schools in Plains, Georgia. There were separate schools for the white children and the black children, but that didn't seem strange to him, even though his playmates were all black children. It was just the way things were. He graduated from the United States Naval Academy with a bachelor of science degree in 1946. Later he studied nuclear physics at Union College. In the navy he became a lieutenant (senior grade) and worked on the development of the nuclear submarine program.

When Jimmy Carter's father died in 1953, he resigned from the navy to return to Plains and take over his father's business, which sold farm supplies and fertilizer. He also farmed his own land. By then he was married to Rosalyn, who was also from Plains. She kept the books while he did the manual labor.

Soon after Carter returned to Georgia he became chairman of the county school board, and then he became the first president of the Georgia Planning Commission. In 1962 he was elected to the Georgia state senate, and in 1971 he became the governor of Georgia.

Three years later he announced that he was running for president of the United States on the Democratic ticket. He and his friends and family worked full-time for two years traveling around the country so that people could get to know him. He also wrote a book that explained his beliefs and his plans to make government "competent and compassionate." He believed that the government should respond to the American people's expectations. Jimmy Carter was elected president in 1976.

When President Carter came to Washington, D.C., he brought many of the people he had worked with in Georgia with him. He was determined to have honesty in government, and he knew and trusted these people. It was an unpopular move with the establishment in Washington, D.C., however. During his term, Carter worked hard to control inflation and lower unemployment. During his presidency there was an increase of nearly eight million jobs and a decrease in the budget deficit. Unfortunately, inflation and interest rates were about as high as they had ever been. Although he was working to reduce inflation and interest rates, Carter's policies caused a short recession.

President Carter achieved many things during his presidency. He established a national energy policy, he worked on deregulating the trucking and airline industries, and he worked on reforming the civil service. Other things that he concentrated on domestically included building up the Social Security system and appointing more Hispanics, women, and blacks to government jobs than ever before. He was also concerned about the environment, and he tried to set standards to improve it.

In international affairs Carter had some huge accomplishments. He hosted a group of meetings that achieved the Camp David agreement of 1978, which was crucial to peace in the Middle East. He helped to bring cooperation between Israel and Egypt. He established full diplomatic relations with the People's Republic of China and got the Panama Canal treaties ratified. President Carter also negotiated the SALT II (strategic arms limitation talks) nuclear limitation treaty with the Soviet Union. And throughout all of his other work, he always was protecting human rights all over the world.

Carter was not reelected in 1980, which was a real blow to him. But instead of retiring to his farm in Plains, Jimmy Carter has spent the twenty-five years since his presidency actively working to promote democracy all over the world. He started the Carter Center, and through it he travels throughout the world to help resolve conflicts and protect human rights. He has started and supported programs to prevent disease and to help health and agriculture advance in the developing world.

President Carter is also an active writer. He has published many books of memoirs, poetry, and history and even a work of fiction. He still teaches Sunday school at his church in Plains, Georgia. He enjoys tennis, skiing, cycling, and jogging and is an avid woodworker and fly fisherman.

Jimmy Carter's work at the Carter Center has earned him world-wide recognition and respect. Everyone I have talked to has high regard for him and his accomplishments, regardless of what they think of his politics. He is known throughout the world as a pro-moter of democracy and human rights. He has traveled all over the world monitoring elections to make sure that they are honest. President Carter was awarded the Nobel Peace Prize in 2002 "in recog-nition of his untiring effort to find peaceful solutions to international conflicts, to advance democracy and human rights, and to promote economic and social development."

How Will Got the Interview

Jimmy Carter's dedication to peace is a continuing inspiration to me. It seems to me that he is a leader with ideals and the perseverance to work energetically toward those ideals in order to make the world a better place—to bring fairness, equality, decency, and basic human rights to all people. I wanted to interview Carter because he is a peace hero for the world.

Of course, Jimmy Carter also keeps pretty busy. I bombarded the U.S. senators from Utah and Idaho with letters asking them to inter-cede for me. I wrote to the Carter Center in Atlanta. I wrote to his home in Plains, Georgia. I even found out who the leader of my church's congregation was in Americus (the nearest town to Plains that has a branch of my church) and wrote him a letter asking if he would intercede for me.

Nothing worked. I got a nice letter from my senator gently sug-gesting that maybe President Carter was too involved with other more important things to be able to meet with me.

My grandfather is very active in state politics with the Democratic Party. He suggested that I try writing to his old friend, the retired senator from Utah, Ted Moss. So I did. Senator Moss sent me a copy of the letter he sent to President Carter along with my letter to him. It basically said that my family members were hardworking Demo-crats and it would be nice if President Carter could help me.

Amazingly, it worked! President Carter's secretary called me and said that President Carter didn't have time to meet with me, but that if I would send my written questions to her, President Carter would answer them and send them back.

So I sent my questions, and he replied. Instead of answering all my questions, he suggested I read his books, *Why Not the Best?* and *Always a Reckoning*. I did read them and thought they were tremendous. I guess some of my questions were thought-provoking for him, because he said in his letter that he hoped I would attend his Sunday school class in Plains someday, so he could ask *me* some tough questions as well!

I still wish I could have met him in person. I feel such respect and appreciation for him.

◆

Interview

VIA PERSONAL LETTER, JUNE 17, 1996

WILL: You have said that your favorite book is *Let Us Now Praise Famous Men* by James Agee. So I checked it out of the library. It is about these poor sharecropper families in the 1930s in the South. It was amazingly depressing. You've said that you liked the book because it was like an analysis of the way you grew up. In your book *Why Not the Best?* you stated that your life on a farm during the Great Depression more nearly resembled farm life of fully two thousand years ago than farm life today. Tell me a little about your home when you were about my age.

JIMMY CARTER: We drew water from a well in the yard, and every day of the year we had the chore of keeping extra bucketfuls in the kitchen and on the back porch, combined with the constant wood-sawing and chopping to supply the cooking stove and fireplaces. In every bedroom was a slop jar (chamber pot) that was emptied each morning into the outdoor privy. This small shack had a large hole for adults and a lower and smaller one for children; we wiped with old newspapers or pages torn from Sears, Roebuck catalogs. These were much better facilities than those I knew when I was with the other families on the place, who squatted behind bushes and wiped with corncobs or leaves.

It was a great day for our family in 1935 (I was eleven) when Daddy purchased from a mail-order catalog and erected a windmill with a high wooden tank and pipes that provided running water for the kitchen and a bathroom with toilet.

Our artificial light came from kerosene lamps. We had a battery-powered radio in the front room that we used sparingly, and only at night, as we all sat around looking at it during "Amos and Andy," "Fibber McGee and Molly," "Jack Benny," or "Little Orphan Annie."

An almost unbelievable change took place in our lives when electricity came to the farm. The continuing burden of pumping water, sawing wood, building fires in the cooking stove, filling lamps with kerosene, and closing the day's activity with the coming of night—all these things changed dramatically.

I have vivid memories of how cold it was in winter. The worst job was getting up in the morning to start a fire going somewhere in the frigid house.

Almost all our food was produced in our pasture, fields, garden, and yard. Nothing went to waste around our house, and we were expected to eat whatever was prepared and to clean our plates before leaving the table.

Corn was our staple grain, and rarely would we have a meal without grits, lye hominy, roasting ears, or one of the half-dozen recipes for corn bread. We always had chickens available, whether hens or fryers, and it was usually my job to catch and kill them so they could be dressed and then baked, fried, or made into a pie.

WILL: Tell me about some of your heroes when you were about my age.

JIMMY CARTER: A black man in our little town of Archery enjoyed the highest social and—our community believed—financial status.

He was African Methodist Episcopal Bishop William Decker John-
son, whose primary religious responsibilities encompassed five Mid-
western states. There was no doubt that he dominated the
consciousness of everyone in the church, and, at least during the ser-
mon, the sense of being brothers and sisters in Christ wiped away
any thoughts of racial differences. To me, he seemed the epitome of
success and power. Of no less importance to me, he retained his close
ties with Archery and the people who lived there. I still go by his rel-
atively modest grave on occasion and wonder how much my own
ambitions were kindled by these early impressions.

The approval of my father has always been one of my most vivid
memories. My father was the center of my life and the focus of my
admiration when I was a child. He was a serious and sometimes stern
businessman, but often lively and full of fun with his friends and
with the men and women who lived on our farm. On the occasions
when he hugged me, just being there enfolded in my father's arms
was one of the most unforgettable moments of my life. As a child I
was inclined to consider him omniscient and infallible. He was
always my best friend.

My own personal favorite among great American presidents is
Harry Truman. He revered the presidency itself, and he used it in an
aggressive fashion. The long-range concepts he had of foreign inter-
relationships, the courage he showed when he dealt with the firing
of General Douglas MacArthur during the Korean War—all these
are things that I admire. I don't believe that Harry Truman was ever
corrupt. He was meticulously honest. I had his sign on my desk,
"The buck stops here." It was my government; I took responsibility
for it.

WILL: What were your life goals, dreams, and ambitions when you
were about my age?

JIMMY CARTER: My greatest ambition was to be valuable around
the farm and to please my father. My big ambition was to plow a
mule, but this task was usually reserved for full-grown men, since it
required enough size and strength to hold the plow handles and at
the same time to manage the mule with plow lines going to the bri-

dle bit. When I was finally able to do it, I've rarely had a more satisfying experience.

After this, my desire to learn everything possible about farming
was even more intense, but I had to be able to do a man's work. This
equaled any other ambition I've ever had in my life. It involved learning how to plant and cultivate a crop.

By the time I was sixteen, I knew about all the chores that had to
be performed on the farm, was familiar with the animals and
machinery, and was fairly proficient in carpentry and in the skills of
a blacksmith. Although the farm was my most likely future, I had
developed a different goal.

No one of our Carter ancestors had ever finished high school, and
it seemed then that any college opportunities were limited to the two
free military institutions, West Point and Annapolis. Uncle Tom
Gordy had joined the navy when he was quite young and made a
lifetime career of it. He was my distant hero. So, from the time I was
five years old, I would always say that someday I would be going to
Annapolis. The vague image of someday being on a ship became my
dream.

As I approached graduation from high school, the Naval Academy became almost an obsession in our family. If I slacked off at all
from my schoolwork, one of my parents was sure to say, "You'll
never go to Annapolis this way!"

WILL: What books did you enjoy reading when you were around
my age? I know that you read *War and Peace* when you were about
twelve. Was that your favorite book at that point?

JIMMY CARTER: The senior nurse at the hospital where my mother
worked was Miss Gussie Abrams. She was a close friend of my parents and was my godmother. On my eighth birthday she gave me a
matched leather-bound set of Victor Hugo's works and a twenty-vol-
ume set of *The Outline of Knowledge*. This is still one of my treas-
ured possessions. My usual request to Santa was for books.

When I was about twelve years old my teacher called me in and
stated that she was ready for me to read *War and Peace*. I was happy
with the title because I thought that finally Miss Julia had chosen for

me a book about cowboys and Indians. I was appalled when I checked the book out of the library because it was about fourteen hundred pages long, written by the Russian novelist Tolstoy, and of course not about cowboys at all. It turned out to be one of my favorite books, and I have read it two or three times since then.

Even as a grammar-school child, I read books about the navy and Annapolis. I wrote to ask for the entrance requirements, not revealing my age, and I almost memorized the little catalog when it came. Then I planned my studies and choice of library books accordingly.

WILL: How have you made the important decisions in your life?

JIMMY CARTER: When I was a younger person I was always very eager to do the most advanced and sometimes quite dangerous things. As soon as our country had the idea of having atomic power to propel submarines I was one of the first ones to volunteer and was one of the very earliest submarine officers to go into the atomic power program.

I have never been afraid of taking a chance or facing the possibility of defeat, and I've always done the best I could. I've never been particularly grieved or disheartened when I tried something and it wasn't completely successful if I had done my best. I've had an underlying stability in my life derived from my community, family, and religious beliefs. There hasn't been any one dramatic thing in my life that has transformed me. One of the things that shaped my life was realizing that I have one life to live on this earth, and I ask God frequently not to let me waste it and to let my life be beneficial for my fellow human beings in His kingdom.

Two hundred years from now when people consider my name, I would like them to equate it with peace and human rights.

WILL: What would you like to tell kids my age and a little younger?

JIMMY CARTER: I think the most important thing to teach is that we should not accept unnecessary limits in our own lives. The most severe limit is most often the one we place on ourselves by not striving for greatness, or by not attempting to utilize our talent, ability, and opportunities to the utmost. A refusal to meet life's challenges with vigor and determination can severely restrict one's vitality.

Society has to be careful how it defines winners and losers. The leaders in our society who do the defining tend to assume that winners are those who are most similar to us, who have fame, material wealth, and some publicized success. But there are others in life who are perhaps even greater winners in the eyes of God: those who are humble, self-sacrificial, unselfish, who care about others, and who are filled with charity or love. Quite often these people are not known, are not famous, don't have a notable accomplishment in their lives, and have little material wealth. I'm always cautious about deciding that people are losers, even though they haven't reached the same level of achievement that I've defined for my own life. The so-called winners must be sure that their actions don't denigrate the accomplishments of others. It's not always proper for so-called successful people to look down on unsuccessful people and ask, "What's wrong with you people?"

WILL: What do you hope to accomplish with the rest of your life?

JIMMY CARTER: I hope that I'll continue to learn.

5

Orson Scott Card

Orson Scott Card is a prolific writer. In addition to having more than sixty books published, including mainstream novels, religious novels, and fantasy novels, he has written movie screenplays, full-length plays, musical plays, hymns, and the scripts for animated videos. He has also written textbooks on writing, poetry, columns in magazines, and the script for the Hill Cumorah Pageant, which is presented every year in Palmyra, New York. His series of books that includes *Ender's Game* is read in many high schools.

In Redmond, Washington, in 1951, Card was born into a family who loved to read and write. His parents were both teachers; his mother was talented in music and drama, while his father had talent in the visual arts. This created a very artistic environment.

The family lived in Utah, Arizona, California, and Washington during Card's childhood. He has said that it was a happy time for him, although he was better at getting along with adults than with children and so was often lonely. He was also very intelligent and enjoyed individual activities such as wandering through the Arizona desert or exploring the woods, creeks, and orchards near where he lived in California. He enjoyed shooting baskets by himself but lacked the skill to play basketball with other boys. He liked to hike and climb by himself. Team sports became more important as he grew older, and so early on he associated less with boys and more with girls, who at that time were not involved in organized sports. He enjoyed talking with girls because they didn't judge him.

Scott Card played the tuba and the French horn during the time his family lived in California, and he marched in the school band in Arizona playing either the sousaphone or the E-flat alto horn. He was also a voracious reader. He rode his bicycle to the library and read every book in the children's section before he started in on the adult sections.

When Card was a theater major in college he started writing plays. He didn't have a driver's license, and so he did most of his writing on lined notebook paper while he was sitting around in odd places waiting for his father to pick him up and take him home. At one point he took a two-year break from college to live in Brazil and act as a missionary for his church. He has a bachelor's degree from Brigham Young University and a master's degree from the University of Utah, and he started work at Notre Dame on a Ph.D.

Scott Card has been married to his wife, Kristine Allen, since they were in college. They have five children: Geoffrey, Emily, Charles, Zina Margaret, and Erin Louisa, named for favorite authors Geoffrey Chaucer, Emily Brontë and Emily Dickinson, Charles Dickens, Margaret Mitchell, and Louisa May Alcott, respectively. His youngest child died the day she was born, and his son Charles Benjamin Card was born with cerebral palsy and could neither speak nor walk. Card dedicated the book *Maps in a Mirror* "to Charlie Ben, who can fly." He has explained that this refers to a game the two of them played in which Card threw his son up in the air and caught him, again and again. Charlie died at age seventeen.

Card usually has a dozen or more ideas for books in his mind. He jots down ideas as he researches and reads. An idea will slowly grow in his mind for three to five years, and then Card will write the whole book out in one amazing burst of creativity, which takes about a month of solid typing on his laptop. He says that he does it that way so that he can't forget any of the details that he has written earlier in the book.

The books that Orson Scott Card writes never depend on graphic violence or sex; these may be suggested in his novels but are almost never described. He also almost never uses swear words. He believes that he opens up his books to a larger audience by keeping them clean and also says that he can't bear to write what he wouldn't want to read aloud to his child.

Orson Scott Card's books continue to win an amazing number of awards. Two of the most important book awards are the Hugo Award and the Nebula Award. In 1985 he won both of them. That had never happened before. Then the next year he won both of them again, for a different book! Card insists that he doesn't write toward the awards. He feels that they are out of his hands, and it's like a happy coincidence when he does win one.

At this time Card's books *Ender's Game* and *Ender's Shadow* are being made into a movie by Warner Brothers. Scott Card wrote the first draft of the screenplay, and now Hollywood writers are working on further drafts. There will also be an electronic game that will tie in to the movie's release. *Ender's Game* has been one of the most popular science-fiction novels ever published since it came out in 1985.

Card lives in Greensboro, North Carolina, with his wife and youngest child. He is a professor of writing and literature at Southern Virginia University and offers free writing workshops on his website. He also writes a weekly column called "Uncle Orson Reviews Everything," which is published by the *Rhinoceros Times* in Greensboro and then online. Card has begun writing illustrated novels for the comic series Ultimate Iron Man for Marvel, and he will also be writing the comic book prequels to Advent Rising, a video game that he helped to create.

How Rob Got the Interview

Orson Scott Card was the first hero I interviewed after I took over this project from Will. I made a list of people that I thought fit Will's definition of a hero, and I started writing letters. But I hadn't heard back from anyone. And I had not yet written to Card.

Card was on my list because I really admire the way that his standards and ideals are reflected in his writing. I have gained, and continue to receive, many hours of pleasure and introspection from Card's novels, and I always come away from them feeling like I'm a better person, in some small way. They are also a kind of litmus test for me. If I am carrying a book by Orson Scott Card, almost inevitably someone will come up and start talking to me about it because Card is a favorite of his or hers, too. I've had some great discussions that way and have even met some of my friends that way.

Getting the interview with Card was kind of a fluke. We were eating dinner, and my mom said, "Isn't Orson Scott Card on your list of heroes? He has a book signing tonight in Orem." So my mom and dad, my two brothers, and I all packed into the car and drove the forty miles south to Orem. On the way Mom suggested that I might want to write down some questions—just in case he wanted to do the interview right then. It seemed unlikely to me, but I wrote down some questions. My dad had already grabbed the tape recorder and camera.

There was no line in front of Card's table. So I went up and told him about my project. He seemed interested and supportive. I asked if I could go ahead and ask him my questions. He was doubtful that it would work. I think he kept expecting that lots of people would show up at any minute. But he agreed that we could get started with the questions and then just quit when it got busy. Well, I don't know what lucky star I was under that night, but it never did get busy, and I was able to ask all my questions. I was ecstatic.

I've gone to several of Card's book signings since then. I've always had to wait in line an hour or so for my turn, and then I've had about one minute to talk to him while he was signing my book. I don't know why that first book signing was different. I think the weather was bad—maybe that kept people home. Or maybe I was just lucky.

And then six years went by. I was able to have several more interviews with other heroes. And I even found an agent, and then a publisher! So I started trying to get all the interviews in shape. When I got to this one, I was frustrated to see how many things I still wished I had asked him. I wrote to Card's official website, asking if he would be in Salt Lake any time soon. Several months later, he had a book signing in Salt Lake. It was just one month before my finished manuscript was due at the publisher. Again, I heard about it only a couple of days before the event. So I hurriedly wrote to Card at the official address, and also via his brother who lives in the area (in case he was staying with his brother), and then went to the book signing.

This signing was not deserted as the first one had been. There was no way Card could give me more than a minute of his time, and he was already on his way out of town. We did take a new photo of the two of us, and he agreed to follow up via e-mail.

So—and this is extraordinary—I sent him the questions. And the very next day the answers showed up in my e-mail. Can you imagine that? What a thoughtful and understanding person, to put his own projects to one side to make himself so accessible to me.

———◈———

Interview

DESERET BOOKSTORE, OREM, UTAH, AUGUST 10, 1999

ORSON SCOTT CARD: OK, Robert, hit it!

ROB: OK. As you know, my book is about my personal heroes and what they were like when they were my age. Who were your heroes when you were ten to fourteen?

ORSON SCOTT CARD: When I was about eleven my parents had given me Bruce Catton's Army of the Potomac trilogy for my birthday. In reading that, it added to my already great interest in the Civil War. At that time, if I'd had to pick a hero it probably would have been Robert

E. Lee or Stonewall Jackson. Those were the heroes. But I don't really remember having "hero" heroes, you know, where you think, "Oh, this person's great; I want to be just like him." There were people I admired, but nobody that I was interested in emulating. I was so arrogant at that age that I assumed that I would make my own path.

I know that all my life Joseph Smith has been an important figure in my life. His writings and his translating work on the *Book of Mormon*—again, does that count as being a hero? I don't know, because his life was difficult, and I really didn't have any interest in trying to do the same thing, to follow his path in that way.

In fact, on that score, I'd probably have to point to my dad, because he was a great man that I wanted to be like. But even there, he was an artist and a photographer, and I wasn't. So the concept of hero is one that I have never been that comfortable with in terms of saying, "Who's your hero?"

I wish that I could tell you more. Mark Twain. Come to think of it, it's Mark Twain that I've actually emulated. And he's the one that wrote *The Prince and the Pauper*. At that age (I'm having to remember here) I was an intense Anglophile. I had read *The Prince and the Pauper* when I was about eight, and so I had this thing about English history. So maybe, in the back of my mind, I had Mark Twain there as my hero—because he wrote the book that made me fall in love with England. Even though now, of course, I know that *The Prince and the Pauper* is so grossly inaccurate about English history. But, you know, what the heck! At the time I absolutely loved it. And so he did set me to dreaming, and maybe he is responsible for setting my feet on the path that I've been on.

You know, when I was much older, then I did have a hero—Shakespeare. I was grimly determined to be to my people what Shakespeare was to his. But, who knows? That was when I was eighteen or nineteen. I've grown up since then and discovered that that's a hard role to fill.

ROB: Do you think your heroes would be proud of what you've accomplished?

ORSON SCOTT CARD: You know, some of them would be completely uninterested in what I've accomplished. But Mark Twain was definitely generous to younger writers, and I think that even if he wasn't thrilled with what I wrote, because he fancied himself an atheist, and my stuff is definitely not of that stripe, nevertheless I think that he'd at least be kind to me.

Shakespeare—we don't know if he was kind to people. But everything that we know of his life suggests that he was a man of generosity. When he was older it appears that he developed some kind of palsy so that he was unable to write. So he had a collaborator that he worked with. And the very fact that he was willing to work with a collaborator suggests that maybe he would have looked at my work and said, "Well, good for you young man."

ROB: Who are your heroes today and why?

ORSON SCOTT CARD: Today one of my greatest heroes is my son Geoffrey. He is the most honest person that I know. He does not lie. Period. No matter what. He never protects himself from the consequences of his own actions by concealing what he's done. And he is a fine and generous man.

And then there's my daughter Emily, who, despite great tribulations has become a marvelously empathetic and good and generous person. She has great talent that she magnifies.

And then there's my son Charlie Ben, who has cerebral palsy and manages to be amazingly patient and cheerful through that. He is just a great kid. So, even though he can't speak, I look at him with profound admiration.

And then there's my wife, who takes care of him. It sounds like I'm just saying my family, but those are the people that I admire most.

And then there's my daughter Zina, who is the most brilliant child ever born; just ask her, she'll tell you! But she is extraordinary. It is just a joy to watch her and see who she is becoming. But that's who I know best, so that's who I'm most likely to admire as a hero.

But then, if you talk about people who aren't in my family, I'll tell you, Dave Wolverton [a former neighbor] is a man that I greatly admire—both his talent and great life, and the way he deals with other people. He's a guy who had a real varied batch of jobs. He's been a prison guard, for heaven's sake. But I've seen him be unfailingly good to other people. But that's the standard that I judge people by—great accomplishments. Famous people, I'm not impressed by that. In my own way I've had my own dose of fame. I realize how little that has to do with whether you actually matter in the world. What I look for is just people who are good. And you don't find them by reading *People* magazine. You find good people by looking around you among the common people that you know and seeing who is kind and generous.

ROB: Back to when you were my age, what were your hobbies, and when did you know that you wanted to be a writer?

ORSON SCOTT CARD: I didn't know that I wanted to be a writer until I was in college. My hobby—my favorite thing to do was read. I read as much as I possibly could. Beyond that, I loved hanging out with friends, hanging out in the creeks and orchards and woods around where we lived in Santa Clara, and when I was older, in Mesa, Arizona, going out in the desert with my dad. We would carry .22s and pretend we were shooting rabbits, but even if we saw one we always missed, and I don't think that we were really that bad of shots. Nobody wanted to have a rabbit die because we wanted to go out in the desert. I don't know if you can call that a hobby; but it was a great pleasure.

I never collected anything, except books. For a while there I had thousands and thousands of books, but we started giving away the ones we knew we were never going to read again. So what I have is a great reference library, and then the books that have special meaning to me. I never collected stamps. I never collected rocks. My interests just kept changing too much.

I did have a brief time where I was a Civil War buff. I had a time when I was deeply into Anglophilia. And those two things have translated into a lifelong interest in history.

I wouldn't call it a hobby because I thought it was going to be my life's work. But I thought I was going to work in theater—acting, directing, that sort of thing.

But, when I was your age, singing was a hobby. My mom would play the piano and I'd sing. We'd sing in the car. The whole family sang.

ROB: Do you believe in God?

ORSON SCOTT CARD: Absolutely.

ROB: When you start writing a book do you know all the things that will happen?

ORSON SCOTT CARD: I have a plan, but I also feel free to wing it as I go along. That's why the Alvin Maker series has seven volumes instead of the three in the outline. I'm still following the outline; it's just that there's a whole bunch of other stuff that came up along the way.

ROB: Are many of your characters based on yourself, members of your family, or friends?

ORSON SCOTT CARD: Never, except with one big exception, which is the story *Lost Boys*. It is based on my family in 1983, the first year that we lived in Greensboro, North Carolina. Now, it's not absolutely based on us. But the characters are meant to be like us. That's the only exception. Everybody else, I make up. And I don't ever base them on my friends, or even my enemies. It's just that my friends I don't know well enough to write about. But my made-up characters, I know perfectly.

ROB: How long does it take you to write a book?

ORSON SCOTT CARD: I usually think about it for years, and plot and outline and contemplate things. But the typing time—I usually get started and work on it for a week, or a week and a half, then let it sit for a few weeks, or a month, or two months. Then I go back and finish it all in three weeks.

ROB: Do you have a set schedule for your work?

ORSON SCOTT CARD: No. When I'm working on a book I write and write and write, until I can't write any more that day. When I'm done with the book I try to avoid writing as much as possible, until the checks start bouncing, and then I go back to work.

ROB: What were your favorite books when you were my age?

ORSON SCOTT CARD: What's your exact age right now?

ROB: Eleven.

ORSON SCOTT CARD: So that's sixth grade?

ROB: Fifth.

ORSON SCOTT CARD: Fifth grade was when I was reading Bruce Catton's Army of the Potomac trilogy. That would have been my favorite book at that time. And I also read *The Rise and Fall of the Third Reich* then. My sister got it in college, and I was too young to read it, emotionally, but I could read it intellectually, obviously. But it was profoundly disturbing, but a very important book to me. Calling it a favorite is kind of weird, but it was very important to me.

ROB: What did you want to do when you were my age?

ORSON SCOTT CARD: When I was your age I wanted to be a doctor. That lasted for another couple of years, and then I wanted to be an archaeologist.

ROB: Oddly enough, doctor has flown through my mind a couple of times.

ORSON SCOTT CARD: That's good. It's a good thing to do. People actually want you to do it, you know? Whereas with fiction writing, it's really an outrageous thing to think that I can make stuff up and make people pay to read it. That's weird. I don't understand why that works. But I'm glad it does.

ROB: Have you published anything that you would be embarrassed to have your children or your bishop read?

ORSON SCOTT CARD: Nothing that I would be embarrassed to have my bishop read. But I don't always write things that would be appropriate for children, so sometimes I would want them to grow up before they read it. But no, everything I've written I stand by.

[At this point, flash ahead six years, to when Card kindly answered some more questions.]

ROB: You have said that the feeling of not fitting in, when you were my age, of feeling like you were intellectual rather than being physically active, and that the closeness to girls and participation in the society of girls explains a lot about the subjects you write about and the types of people you understand best. Can you give me a couple of examples of characters that are like you remember being when you were my age?

ORSON SCOTT CARD: Being physically inactive did not help me as a writer; it made it harder for me to understand people who *are* athletic. Not till I began running and other athletic activities in my late forties did I begin to understand something of the appeal. . . . And being close to girls going through school did not lead me to write characters who were similar to *me*; it led me to be better at writing about girls! As a general rule, I don't consciously base any characters on me. The only one who is like me is Step Fletcher in *Lost Boys*.

ROB: I turned sixteen this summer and got my driver's license just as soon after that as I possibly could. I know that you didn't get your driver's license until you were twenty-three. Why is that?

ORSON SCOTT CARD: Utah required that kids take drivers ed before getting a license. But my high school—a private one, Brigham Young High—didn't offer drivers education in the curriculum. So I had to take a night class at the local trade-tech to become eligible for a license. Yet their classes were held at exactly the same time as all the play rehearsals I wanted to be involved with. So I kept signing up, attending the first class, and never attending another. Then I went on my mission at age twenty, and even when I got home, I was frantically busy with my new job and my theater company. Only when my girlfriend (now my wife) told me she was tired of driving us on our dates did I finally take the time to finish a course and get my license—a week before my twenty-third birthday.

ROB: You have stated that young writers should not waste their time and money going to college but instead should get a real job, have a real life, write their brains out, and read a lot, preferably nonfiction and things that they don't know much about. Do you still believe that? You, yourself, earned a bachelor's degree, a master's degree, and began work on a doctorate. In addition, you have taught at the university level. Why this lack of loyalty to academia?

ORSON SCOTT CARD: On the contrary—I think college is a wonderful experience. What I tell young writers is that if they want training to be novelists then college is a waste of time, because almost no one in the colleges knows how to teach the skills that can actually be taught (they try to teach the ones that aren't worth teaching, like "style"). The best training is to write your brains out—you learn more from writing a hundred thousand words than you do from taking a college course in writing.

The classes I teach aren't a waste of time—I actually *do* know how to teach the skills that can be taught, like viewpoint, story structure, rigorous ideation, etc. Even so, it's more vital for a writer to keep his nonacademic connections—to have "nonintellectual" friends so the writer doesn't come to believe that noncollege people are somehow "other" and then write contemptuously or patronizingly of them. At the same time, in today's society you need a college degree to get a decently lucrative job so you can support a family while trying to win a place as a writer. So as long as the writer is not confused and remembers that college is about getting a good job, *not* about training as a writer, then there's nothing wrong with going to college.

ROB: Thank you very much. I don't know if you can appreciate how grateful I am. Have a great day!

———

6

Yo-Yo Ma

Yo-Yo Ma is the finest cello player in the world and might well be the most famous musician alive today. People describe his music as fiery and exciting. Ma has made recordings of almost all the classical music ever written for the cello. He likes to try new things, including playing music that was originally written for another instrument. He loves to explore new music from different countries, and since 1998 he has been working on a project he started called the Silk Road Project, which is working to preserve the music of the countries that lie along the ancient Silk Road trade route between Asia and Europe.

Among the more than fifty recordings that Ma has made, there are many that are of classical music. But there are also ones of American Appalachian music, jazz, Indian music, Argentine tangos, and many more. He even owns a special cello, called a hypercello, which is a computerized instrument designed especially for him.

Yo-Yo Ma was born in Paris, France, in 1951. His father, Dr. Hiao-Tsiun Ma, was a musicologist who taught violin and composition. His mother, Ya-Wen Lo (Marina Ma), was a mezzo-soprano singer. His parents had emigrated from China to France many years earlier. His family was very poor and sometimes did not have enough money to buy wood to burn to keep warm.

When he was just four years old, Ma's father started teaching him how to play the cello. He used a cello that was just one-sixteenth as large as a regular cello. His father used new methods that he made up to teach him, and he showed amazing talent. His father insisted that he work very hard, and Ma had his first public performance when he was just five years old.

When Ma was seven years old he moved with his family to New York City. Soon, with his older sister on the piano, he gave a performance for President John F. Kennedy and another performance with the conductor Leonard Bernstein that was on television all over the country.

Although Ma's parents had always taught him at home, when he was nine years old, he started attending a precollege program at the Julliard School of Music in New York City. He studied there for six years. By the time Yo-Yo Ma was seventeen, he could have begun a full-time concert career, but instead he enrolled at Harvard College in Cambridge, Massachusetts. While he was there he took classes in subjects he had never had the opportunity to study before, like Chinese history, fine arts, German literature, and Russian novelists. He also, of course, studied the cello and gave concerts all over the world.

Ma still lives near Harvard University with his wife and son and daughter, although he is traveling almost half the days of the year so that he can give concerts. Ma has a wonderful sense of play and whimsy and has a reputation for playing practical jokes. Sometimes he has gotten into pillow fights on airplanes.

Ma has been awarded many prizes for his cello playing. In 2001 he was given the National Medal of Arts. He has also won fifteen

Grammy Awards and one Latin Grammy. He won the Glen Gould Prize in 1999 and the Avery Fisher Prize in 1978.

Ma enjoys studying the role that music plays in people communicating with each other. In order to understand better how it works, he has studied music from all over the world. He has learned about the music of the Kalahari bush people in Africa and about the instruments and music of China and India.

Ma owns four cellos. Two of them are new, and two are very old and valuable. One is a Montagnana cello from Venice, Italy, worth two and a half million dollars. It made headlines all over the world in 1999 when Ma forgot it and left it behind in a taxicab in New York City. Eventually the police found it in a taxi garage in Queens, New York. Ma calls that cello "Petunia." Another of his cellos is the famous Davidoff Stradivarius made in 1712. Ma has named it "Sweetie Pie."

In 1980 Yo-Yo Ma had surgery on his back for scoliosis, which is curvature of the spine. Before the operation the doctors told him that he might not be able to play the cello after the surgery. Ma had the operation anyway and had to stay in a cast for six months. After he recovered he discovered that he was two inches taller.

How Rob Got the Interview

I think I first became aware of Yo-Yo Ma when I saw the movie *Crouching Tiger, Hidden Dragon*. I told my parents how wonderful I thought the music was, and they told me that the cellist was Yo-Yo Ma and that they frequently played his tapes in the car when we were driving. So then I realized that I had actually listened to a lot of his playing, without realizing who it was I was listening to.

I don't remember how I came to consider Yo-Yo Ma as a hero. I have a great-aunt who plays violin with the Utah Symphony Orchestra. Maybe she is the one that suggested him to me. At any rate, I started reading about him, and I really liked what I was finding out. I especially liked the fact that after living such a structured, rigid childhood, he went to Harvard University where he wore a black leather motorcycle jacket and took whatever classes seemed interesting to him, without bothering to follow any kind of a major at first.

I wrote letters to Ma's agent and to the different recording companies that he has recorded music with. I tried to get contact information from the office of the Utah Symphony, without much success. I talked to my uncle, who was at Harvard at about the same time, hoping he might have known Ma or might know someone who did know him at that time.

Then I heard that Ma was coming to Salt Lake to perform with the Utah Symphony. My dad and I tried to buy tickets, but the concert was already sold out, so we bought standing-room-only tickets.

I asked my great-aunt who plays with the symphony if she would please hand a letter from me to Ma at a break during rehearsal. She was kind but adamant that she never bothered the guest artists. She said they were always being bombarded by people wanting to meet them and thought it was courteous to just leave them alone. She did say that if we met her backstage after the concert, maybe we could shake Ma's hand.

I loved the concert. It was the first classical concert I'd ever attended. It was just fabulous. The precision and accuracy, the whole atmosphere just blew my mind.

Afterward we walked backstage. There were a lot of people, and there was a line forming to meet him. Dad and I got in line, and my aunt Frances joined us there. We waited a long time, and finally it was my turn to shake Ma's hand. I introduced myself, and he recognized the name and said, "Oh. You're the one that wrote me the letter." So, I guess Aunt Frances had decided to give it to him after all.

He said that he'd be happy to have me interview him, but he didn't set anything up. I hung around the house the next few days, in case someone called to set up the interview, but no one did. I figured that he had probably just been polite, and that was that.

More than a month later my mom answered the phone at our house, and it was Ma's assistant. She said that Ma wanted to do the interview and asked whether the next day would be all right. Mom wasn't about to disagree, and they set up a time for Ma to telephone me.

I don't include the beginning of our conversation here, because Ma spent about ten minutes asking me about what I was doing, what I was interested in. I was amazed that such a busy, successful, and important person would spend so much time wanting to know about me. I even wondered how it had become turned around—it seemed like he was interviewing me.

I think that Ma is one of the most exciting musicians of our time. He affects everyone around him. He creates a feeling of celebration wherever he goes. That is why I chose Yo-Yo Ma as a hero. He is an amazing musician and changes people's lives with his beautiful music, but even more important, he is an amazing human being. He has made the kind of decisions for his own life that he talks about in the interview—to allow himself to be vulnerable and to celebrate all the different parts of life.

Interview

BY PHONE, AUGUST 22, 1999

ROB: As you know, my book is about heroes. Who were your heroes when you were about my age?

YO-YO MA: When I was eleven? Well, I think I admired my sister a lot. She is four years older than I am, and she just knew a lot of things. I thought she was amazing. She played piano. We would play things together. She played violin. She was a much better student than I was. If I had trouble with things I really would ask her for help. She would always help me out. If I got into trouble I would ask her to bail me out. So that was pretty good.

I had a cello teacher who I felt was really gentle and kind, but he was still a little scary because he was an older person. Adults, you know! I'll tell you! But he was really nice and very soft-spoken and very patient with me. His name was Leonard Rose. What I loved about him was that he was apparently a very shy person, and I was very shy when I was eleven. And he would tell me, "I was like this, too." And he wasn't shy anymore . . . well he was a little shy, and withdrawn sometimes. But basically his saying that "I was sort of like you, but I kind of grew out of it" was incredibly encouraging. It kind of made me feel that it was possible one day not to be so shy. And because I loved his cello playing. It had such a gorgeous sound. And he was trying to ask me to be more extroverted in playing and to get the sound out. He would use terms that were very "sixties," but coming from him it sounded kind of strange. He would say, "Sock it to me, baby!" From someone who is fifty, it sounded really funny. But he really tried, even though he came home from playing concerts and would go straight to teaching. He was always kind of tired when I saw him. It was a heavy load of travel, and he was always exhausted after trips. You know that from your own trips. But he was so dedicated to his students. I really appreciated that. I felt that he was on my side. He was rooting for me. And I think that nothing is more important than having someone, especially if you have contact with one of your heroes, to have them sort of root for you. It's great that they identify something in you, that they say, "You're not just some other kid," but that "I think I recognize this in you. I was like this, and this is what I did about it. And I'm rooting for you because I think you can do it." Boy, is that important!

I think when I was eleven—I'm trying to think—I had a drama teacher that I really liked a lot—Miss Coit. She was great. To me she was a tiny old lady—she probably wasn't really that old. We would do a different Shakespeare play every year. And I just liked hanging around her and helping her set up chairs, and listening to her talk.

I had a gym teacher who actually was a former member of the Bolshoi Ballet. He was Russian, and he was in unbelievable shape. And I'm not a good person at gymnastics, but he'd do all these things on those horses and trapezes, and I just thought that was pretty wild. Of course, I think I loved all these people's stories. He'd talk to me about what life was like in the dance company, and it was fascinating. I just loved listening to my teachers' stories.

ROB: I know that your life was very structured when you were my age, that you never invited friends over to your house to play or went to their houses for sleepovers or anything. When you did have free time you often spent it with more practicing on the cello. Can you explain to me why that was more fun or more satisfying than anything else you could think of to do?

YO-YO MA: A lot of those things were not my decisions, though I think I probably would have enjoyed a lot of them. And I think one of the things that happens, I'm sure it happens when people have certain specific skills, is that often time gets spent on that thing, which means that you can't do something else. As a kid it was very hard to understand that. I chafed under that. I didn't think it was reasonable. Sure, I loved music. I loved the cello. But I wasn't one of those kids that just happily said, "Good, I will do this to the exclusion of everything else." There was always, either expressed or unexpressed, a desire to go and do other things. Or I'd just shut myself in my room and read, or play games by myself. Of course I wanted to see people, but I was also pretty shy. So it was hard to then say, "I really want to go to so-and-so's house because we're best friends."

America was the third country that my parents lived in. They were born in China and spent many years in France, and so they were less clued in to, generally, what parents did. I think it was tough on them to know what to do. What they did know, however, was that they really cared about our education, the good things. But they were less clued in on other aspects of school life.

ROB: Who are your heroes now?

YO-YO MA: Who are my heroes now? Hmm. You know, it's interesting because the heroes that I mentioned to you earlier, you know, family and teachers and people I knew because they were really my world . . . you know, you mentioned Mr. Rogers. Mr. Rogers is actually one of my heroes because—I don't know if you watch Mr.

Rogers—because I think kids don't watch Mr. Rogers after a certain age, right? Your brother watches him, right? I love Mr. Rogers, because he is exactly who he says he is on television. The same guy. The same person, with the same devotion to what he does. And he treats people so well. I admire people who not only do something very well but that they live their life with kindness. And Mr. Rogers definitely is kind to people. As you know, because of his television work, he is recognized everywhere. And so people say, "Oh, you're so wonderful." And there's never a harsh word. He never gets hot and bothered. He just stays in his calm self. So that's one person I do admire a lot.

I think I do admire a lot of people. I admire my wife. She's always, always supportive. She is such an advocate for what our children do, for what I do. She has a really good sense of humor, which gets us through a lot of tight spots, you know. She has a great character. She's always honest, and she's kind, and a generous person. And it's a difficult life, because our life gets pretty complicated. But I really admire the way that she has always, always been there. She is an amazing person.

I think I can't help but absolutely admire Nelson Mandela, although I've never met him and probably never will. This is a person who was in prison for years. Usually if someone puts you in prison for that long, and you get out, you're pretty mad—pretty angry. And from what I know of what he's done, rather than get mad and say, "OK, my turn. I'll put you in jail," he actually thought beyond himself, and I think he tried to take what one would call the high road. When there is so much that he could be justified in being angry about, he actually decided, "You know what? What's best for everybody is this." And he took that course. Boy. I'm not sure most people would be able to be that way. Hooray for him, to be able to choose that course of action, but actually to get rid of whatever anger he feels, so he can act in a fair way.

ROB: I know that you were allowed to watch TV for half an hour each day, and you liked to watch "Little House on the Prairie" and "Daniel Boone." Why were they your favorites?

Yo-Yo Ma: Oh, I don't know. I think, again, it's sort of like, at dinnertime, it was what was on. So it was either that or the news, you know. I loved the character of Daniel Boone—frontiersman, adventurer. I liked his cap. It's more the shows that were on at that hour. I don't think I got to choose too much what I got to see.

Rob: Were you particularly interested in the American West?

Yo-Yo Ma: I love the American West. I think there are many forms of frontier, that the idea of frontier is not just in land, in terms of the West, but you could say going to the bottom of the ocean is a frontier. Going up to the sky to explore the universe is a frontier. And also, for me especially, in my own work, I think the world of a disciplined imagination is definitely a frontier. When you encounter something you're scared of thinking about, when does your imagination say, "Uh-uh, I don't dare think about that anymore"? And why? And in terms of knowledge, where are we going with learning new things? That's another kind of frontier. I think, in some ways, the language of feeling, of compassion, is a frontier, too. Can you really care for one person? Two people? A hundred people? A thousand people? And at what point does it stop being really caring about? What's the maximum that you can feel compassion for? So, in that sense, yes, the American West was a wonderful way of immediately showing, "Yup, it's hard to go on the Oregon Trail. It's hard to go past the Rockies." And boy, there are a lot of courageous people out there.

Rob: Did you have any pets when you were my age?

Yo-Yo Ma: When I was fifteen I had a rabbit. Before, when we were in France we did have two rabbits, and that was great. I love pets.

Rob: I know that you speak at least three languages perfectly. What languages do you think and dream in? And was it the same when you were my age?

Yo-Yo Ma: First of all, I don't speak three languages perfectly. I think my Chinese and French are probably OK, but they are rusty. I don't know what language I dream in—very possibly in English, because that's the language, at this point, of choice. And I know that sometimes, when I'm counting in music, I can count in English, obviously. I think when I remember numbers, probably in Chinese or French, like if I do multiplication, because that's how I learned it. The multiplication tables—I can do it in English also, but certain things are just slightly quicker in the language I learned them. But in dreaming, I don't know. Do you dream in color? Or black and white?

ROB: I have no idea.

YO-YO MA: See? It's hard to remember, isn't it? I have to actually decide, just before I wake up, to say, "OK, what was that dream? What was that dream again?" Probably it depends. If I spend some time in France, then my French can kick in again.

ROB: You seem so American to me, but I realize that you are probably a French citizen, since you were born there. What nationality do you consider yourself?

YO-YO MA: I consider myself human! I am a naturalized American and a proud American citizen. And I really believe in the values of being American. What's great about knowing other countries, other traditions, is that you know different habits, and you know different values. For example, the French love to eat. They love to eat well. They talk about food. You go to the market. You have farmers that have like seventy different kinds of cheese! And they'll show you why this is good, and let you taste this one. So they put a lot of emphasis on developing a vocabulary for describing specific things in, let's say, the cheese, or specific things in describing a kind of bread or something. That's really good because it suddenly makes you focus your taste buds, your vocabulary. You are noticing something around you. I love that. That's just an example. And I think each different place has things like that. And even in America I think there are so many different places that do. And Utah is such a unique place in this country. You go to Maine, or New Orleans, or the Northwest— it's just like different worlds open up. And that's what I love. I love to go to the very specific and say, "Boy, what makes this place tick?"

ROB: I know you were never allowed to play or do any recreational thing that might damage your hands. How did that make you feel when you were twelve or so?

YO-YO MA: Not great. I think I did sports through seventh grade. I loved soccer. But then I was told that I shouldn't play soccer. As an eleven-year-old, I think I was probably much less of a thinking individual than you are. I did what I was told to do. I didn't question it too much. I didn't have enough wherewithal to say, "Hey, wait a minute, I really want to do this, and you're not letting me." I didn't know how to argue in that way. But if I try to think back, I would say, "Gee, I wish I could play sports. I wish I could play soccer. I wish I could do it." But I probably didn't put up a huge fuss.

ROB: Did you ever hate the cello?

YO-YO MA: I think there were times when I loved the cello, but I didn't always think that this was the thing I had to do in my life and the only thing I ever wanted to do. I didn't have that kind of relationship with it. And there were times when I really didn't want to play the cello. I thought I'd rather do other things. And what's funny is that I was about thirty-eight when I finally realized that this is something that I love to do and I'm happy to be a musician. I think that for a lot of my life I thought, "You know, I'd like to do other things, and try other things." But what I realized is that music is so broad. It's sort of like a glue for all kinds of emotions, and for all kinds of ways of thinking—for psychology, for studying culture, for how people interact. To do music well, and knowing about all these things, actually included many of my interests anyway.

ROB: I know when you were twelve music critics were already comparing you to the greatest cellists of all time. How did you feel about that?

YO-YO MA: I don't know. It's always nice to feel that someone thinks you're good at something. But there's a point where it's also not particularly good, because you don't want to peak when you're twelve, you know, or when you're eighteen. "When I was fifteen that was the best year of my life. And now I'm seventy-five years old. Isn't that sad?" You'd like to have a number of peaks. The danger is, when somebody says, "Oh, this is the Michael Jordan of math" or "the Larry Bird of chess playing, or cello playing, or whatever," hey, wait a minute. What is going to happen six years from now? And so I never liked that too much, and I sort of didn't want people to say that.

ROB: Now, your parents were very traditional Chinese. Your grand-mother even had bound feet. How much of the Chinese culture and philosophy is still part of your life?

YO-YO MA: I think that all the influences that I've had are really part of my life because I've just never thought that you want to reject things outright. You just file it away. In terms of upbringing, it's hard to say what you call a cultural value of a certain place. For exam-ple, I'm very close to my wife and children. Family values are cele-brated in many, many cultures. So the fact that we try to have strong family values, is that an American thing? Yup. Is it a French thing? Yup. Is it a Chinese thing? Yup. And strong emphasis on education—is that an American value? Yup. Is it a French value? Yup. Is it a Chi-nese value? Yup. The more I look at any tradition, I actually find that it has resonances in other traditions.

ROB: Do you practice a religion, and, if so, is it a Western or East-ern one?

YO-YO MA: I was brought up Protestant, an Episcopalian. So we go to Memorial Church at Harvard and there is a wonderful minister there. His name is Peter Gomes. He himself is, I think, a Baptist, but he kind of likes the Anglican Church. And also, Memorial Church is sort of an ecumenical place. It's a nondenominational church. Peter Gomes gives great sermons. He's funny. And he always has some-thing really good to say. So I like him. But I'm interested in differ-ent religions, because of all the traveling that we've done. And we're always interested in what people do. I go to Japan a lot, I go see Bud-dhist shrines. I'm interested in how Buddhism went from India to China to Japan. I'm interested in the differences between Protestant and Catholic faiths, and how that developed in different places. For example, all the workers that worked in silk in France were Protestant, but France is a mainly Catholic country. I'm trying to figure out why that is. I haven't found the answer yet. I like to figure things out.

ROB: I know that you were raised to believe that, as a child, you were an extension of your parents and that anything you did was seen as a reflection of your parents, whether it was good or bad. I know that your father was a strong disciplinarian and made all of the decisions for the family. As a father yourself, in what ways have you kept or changed these ideas with your kids?

YO-YO MA: Good question. I think that my father had really good intentions and very good values. I think that he also had a very hard life. I was born when he was, I think, forty-nine years old. That's pretty late. Nicholas, my first child, was born when I was about twenty-seven. I know that the closer you are in age to your kids, the more you can understand where they are coming from in some ways. And you also have more energy. I am not a strong disciplinarian in the family.

My wife, who really has a great feel for family, education, and children, takes the lead in providing the structure of our family. We used to joke around, and she said, "You decide the important things in life. You decide where you're going to play concerts, what repertoire you're going to play, where you're going to travel to, and I decide the less important things—where we're going to live, where the children go to school." Which is, of course, very funny because these are the most important things, you know. And she has such good instincts. So I've really listened to her, and I believe very much in what she has given our children.

We do things a little differently from other families because she and I have both lived in different countries. And so we feel that is one thing that we can pass on to our children—a curiosity about different geographic regions. But we didn't say, "You must speak French at home." We would rather make them curious about something. And, of course, the best way to do it is if my wife and I speak in a different language that they don't understand. They don't like that. They even try to make us stop, or say, "One day I'm going to learn that language!"

We have fun learning about things. So in many ways we have similar values to our parents, but we come from a different generation, a different era. I don't think we do the strict disciplinarian thing, although I think structure, education, and curiosity, learning, knowledge, all that stuff is pretty important.

ROB: Your parents made incredible sacrifices for you and your sister, starting even before you were born, before they realized that you would have a unique talent. Do you feel guilty about all that they gave up so that you and your sister's needs came first?

YO-YO MA: One of the things that I think I've learned is that when you give of yourself, make sure that you give freely. Do not give because you're trying to make a transaction. It's sort of like, Rob, if I said to you, "I did this interview for you, and now what are you doing for me?" I don't think that's fair, because you weren't involved in that transaction.

On the other hand, there was a survival issue in a lot of ways. My parents came from places that were torn apart by war—civil war. My father had the distinct bad luck of experiencing World War II both in China as well as in France, because he was living in France when the Germans invaded Paris. So he had it on both sides. And it's hard for me to fathom, if you grow up like that, what survival means to you. So I feel like they made sacrifices, and made certain decisions that I can only understand from a distance. I may understand more as I get older.

Did they ask me to, therefore, do something for them in return? I think there were certain expectations. I would try to minimize that. I don't think it's good to make people feel guilty. I don't think that's necessarily a healthy emotion. I would much rather, if at all possible, give out of generosity without asking for something back. Otherwise it's just a transaction.

ROB: Are your children musicians?

YO-YO MA: They both learned the piano for a number of years and studied with a wonderful piano teacher. My daughter plays violin, and both my children love to sing. They like musical theater. My son, I think, has a really good voice and likes to sing.

ROB: Now, your parents gave you the European name "Ernest" as well as the Chinese name "Yo." Have you ever used the name "Ernest"?

YO-YO MA: In France I was known as Ernest. France is very much a Catholic country, and a lot of names are given because a child is born on a certain saint's day. I was born on October 7. In China, there was such a great infant mortality rate that often parents would not name their child until he was one month old, because often children didn't survive that long and you didn't want to give a name and then you've bonded with your child, and then your child dies. So they waited, which is the Chinese way of naming the child, until November 7, which fell on the day of Saint Ernest. And so that was why I was given that French name.

ROB: What are your goals now? What do you want to be doing in ten or fifteen years?

YO-YO MA: The goal that remains consistent is to always find a balance between my family life and my working life. My working life always takes me away. And I think that's probably never going to change. The proportions may change, but the idea is to create a balance that is satisfactory to everybody.

I've always been and I will probably continue to be more interested in education of various kinds. And in terms of what I do in music, I think music is a great glue between people, and peoples. I think there's nothing more fun or exciting than working with kids, because if it's exciting then people remember. It's a wonderful thing. So I'll probably be doing more of that.

ROB: You started performing on the cello when you were just four years old. By the time you were seven years old you were performing on national television. Your whole childhood was so different from other kids'. Did you feel like a geek?

YO-YO MA: I felt different. For the longest time I really wanted to know what "normal" meant. The more I lived, the more I realized that yes, there are norms, but they're chosen norms because there really is no absolute norm that you say, "This is it." I wanted to get to a point where you could really speak a common language with common reference points, sort of like saying, "What's your favorite show?" And you go from talking about your favorite show to what's the last movie you've seen, to what sports you like, to whatever. But then you can go on to other things, say, "What are you afraid of?" It took a while to understand all those things. I think it's only in the last ten years or twenty years or so that I could put all these different things together.

ROB: Did the other kids make fun of you?

YO-YO MA: People always made fun of my name. Of course. Who wouldn't? With a name like that it's like, "Hello! Humor time." But I don't think people were nasty to me. I was never in a situation where kids were actively nasty.

ROB: Do you feel it was worth it?

YO-YO MA: I take a page from what pianist Arthur Rubenstein once said. He said that what he tried to do in his life was to live life unconditionally. And so, "worth it" implies that there's a benefit and a cost. You bought this "squeegee-thing." Was it worth it? Was your life worth it? I think I would rather say that what makes life so fantastic is if you embrace it unconditionally, which means in order to experience the richness of it, unfortunately, you have to be very vulnerable to things. If you close yourself off you actually limit what you can receive. If you open yourself totally, you're going to be hurt a lot, because you're sensitive to things. You think about things. You question things. But then the benefit is that you receive a lot. So the point is you're constantly trying to find the balance between the two. With time, and with experience, and a lot of good help from family and friends, I think I've found a way to be as open, as vulnerable, as you can possibly be without hurting yourself drastically.

And so, in that sense, I think it's been worth it. I feel very lucky. But I also think that all of that stuff—it just takes a long time and it takes hard work to put things together in a way that you feel is possible.

ROB: I appreciate your patience. I have just one last question. Do you have any advice you can give to kids my age who feel like they are different from other kids?

YO-YO MA: This maybe goes back to one of the other questions. I think the most important thing for anybody, including kids and adults, is to actually feel that they are known by somebody else the way that they know themselves.

ROB: Well, thank you very much.

YO-YO MA: OK. It's great to talk with you.

ROB: It's great to talk with you.

YO-YO MA: You have a good summer.

ROB: You too. Good-bye.

7

Elouise Cobell

Elouise Pepion Cobell is a member of the Blackfeet Indian Nation. Although she was raised on a ranch in one of the most impoverished areas in the country and had few of the advantages that most people take for granted, she educated herself and achieved momentous things that would eventually help half a million Indian people to have better lives. Incidentally, the name "Blackfeet" is one that exists only in English. In the Blackfeet language (called Piegans) the name of the tribe is "Amskapi Pikuni."

Cobell grew up in a home with no electricity, telephone, or running water. She lived with her parents and nine brothers and sisters on a ranch outside of Browning, Montana, which is very near the Canadian border. This ranch is part of the Blackfeet Indian Reservation. Glacier County, the area surrounding Browning, is the thirty-fifth poorest county in the entire country. Unemployment in the town of Browning is about 70 percent during the winters when there are no construction jobs.

Cobell's family was poor, but they stressed the importance of education. One day when Cobell was just four years old, she went with her father to visit the one-room school near them. Cobell liked it so much that she sat at a desk and would not leave until her father promised that she could come back the next day and start school.

One important tradition in the Blackfeet tribe is telling stories to preserve the tribe's history. As a result, Cobell grew up listening to many stories. One that impressed her was the story of Baker's Massacre in 1870. American soldiers killed two hundred Blackfeet people, and most of them were children and women. The Blackfeet people were ambushed not far from the ranch where Cobell grew up.

She heard other stories about how the tribe's children were sent away from the reservation to go to boarding school for years at a time. Speaking their native language was against the rules at those schools, and children would be punished for doing it.

Through listening to all of these stories, Cobell began to understand that her tribe had often been taken advantage of by the United States government.

Cobell graduated from Great Falls Business College and attended Montana State University for two years. But when her mother became very sick, Cobell returned home to help care for her. She stayed in the Browning area until 1968 when she moved to Seattle, Washington. In Seattle she worked in the accounting department of a local television station and met and married Alvin Cobell, who is also a member of the Blackfeet Nation and was a fisherman off the Alaska coast.

After the birth of their son, Turk, the Cobell family moved back to the ranch near Browning where Cobell had grown up. It is a 320-acre allotment ranch. It's important to note that the Cobells did not technically own this land. Due to the way the reservations were formed, no Indians were allowed to actually own their land. Instead, the government took legal title to the parcels of Indian land and held it in trust for them. The government could sell the land or sell or lease the mineral, grazing, timber, gas and oil, or other rights. The government was legally bound to manage trust accounts, collecting the revenue from them and disbursing that money to the Indians who owned the land.

After moving back to the ranch, Cobell was offered the job of treasurer of the Blackfeet Indian Nation, and she held that position for thirteen years.

During those years Cobell was also the executive director of the Native American Community Development Corporation, a nonprofit part of the Native American Bank. She was one of the organizers of the Blackfeet National Bank, which is the first national bank located on an Indian reservation and owned by a Native American tribe. She also served as the chairperson for the bank.

Cobell had always heard stories from her grandparents and others about how the government had mismanaged the Indian trust monies. As she worked in the bank and as the tribe treasurer, she tried to find answers to the questions tribe members had. She found that by 1932 ninety million acres of "surplus" reservation land had been sold by the federal government. That is about 65 percent of the Indians' land. She discovered that the Indians had very limited knowledge of what they actually owned. Cobell tried to go through the accounting records, but she found more questions than answers.

When she went to the local Bureau of Indian Affairs to get the answers, she was ignored. She kept researching, however, and eventually she and the people working with her found that out of the 238,000 individual Indian trusts they located, 50,000 had no addresses. That meant that the income due to those trusts never left the Treasury, because there was no address to which to send it. Sixteen thousand accounts had no documents at all about them, in spite of the fact that the trusts had been in existence since the 1880s. And another 118,000 trust accounts were missing important papers.

The trusts were supposed to manage the revenues owed to individual Indians from oil leases, timber leases, and other activities. But Cobell found a century of disorganization and dishonesty by the federal government, especially the Interior Department, whose job it is to administer the trusts. She decided that the Interior Department had shortchanged generations of Indians and was continuing to deprive about half a million more—the Indians who are the present beneficiaries of the trusts. She found that even when the money was actually distributed, the Interior Department had not acted in the best interests of the Indians. Indians were often paid only one-tenth as much for leases on their property as whites were for comparable property.

After years of trying to resolve the problems with the Interior Department, in 1997 Elouise Cobell became the lead plaintiff in a lawsuit now known as *Cobell v. Norton* (the plaintiff is the person who initiates a lawsuit). Norton is Gail Norton, who became the secretary of the interior in President Bush's cabinet in January 2001. It is a class-action lawsuit, which means that Cobell is standing in for about five hundred thousand Indians who are the recipients of Indian trust funds. Cobell's goal is to force the government to repay those Indians who have been cheated out of money that was rightfully theirs by the Interior Department and, equally significant, to reform the system so that such a thing can never happen again.

Cobell has won in court every step of the way. Interior officials have repeatedly been placed under sanctions for misconduct and malfeasance, which means that the judge has told them that they are in trouble for being public officials and doing wrong. Both in the trial and then in the appeal that the Interior Department filed (and lost), the judge found that the Departments of the Interior and Treasury engaged in "fiscal and governmental irresponsibility in its purest form" in maintaining and accounting for the trust assets belonging to five hundred thousand individual Indians. In December 2004, the U.S. Court of Appeals ruled that interest is due on all funds owed to Cobell and the other Indians going back to 1887 and that the full accounting of all trust assets must be completed by January 6, 2008. In one opinion, Judge Royce C. Lamberth urged an end to the continuing delay, writing that "the government has not only set the gold standard for mismanagement, it is on the verge of setting the gold standard for arrogance in litigation strategy and tactics."

Today Elouise Cobell spends most of her time working with Native Americans who want to start their own businesses and helping to teach Blackfeet teenagers the basics about money management so that they can never be taken advantage of, as their ancestors were. She also helps her husband on their ranch. One spring, when it was especially cold outside, Cobell was able to save two small newborn calves from freezing to death by warming them up in the shower.

In 1997 Cobell received the Genius Grant from the John D. and Catherine T. MacArthur Foundation's Fellowship Program. She has also been the recipient of many other awards.

How Rob Got the Interview

I first read about Elouise Cobell in an article in *Parade* magazine in 2001 and immediately wrote her a letter. It was only a couple of weeks later that she actually called my house. I was at school and Mom answered the phone. Mom had no idea who this person was when she said, "Hello, I'm Elouise Cobell calling for Robert Hatch."

Cobell agreed to an interview and suggested that instead of our driving all the way to Browning, up near the Canadian border, we meet her in Billings, Montana, where she was participating in a banking conference for middle school students from several reservations.

I loved attending the conference. I learned a lot about banking, and I enjoyed hanging out with Native American kids my age. The first session started with the National Anthem and Pledge of Allegiance, both performed in the Blackfeet language of Piegans. The kids were dressed about the same as I was, but many of the boys had long braids down their backs.

For me, Elouise Cobell is a hero because she has given (so far) thirty years of her life to fixing a wrong that was causing many people a lot of needless suffering. Not only that, but she also helped start a Native American bank and programs such as the one I attended— created to ensure that the next generation of Native Americans is knowledgeable about finances so that this history will never repeat itself.

—◆—

Interview

UNION BUILDING, MONTANA STATE UNIVERSITY, BILLINGS,
MONTANA, OCTOBER 22, 2001

ROB: As you know, my book is about heroes. Who were your heroes when you were my age?

ELOUISE COBELL: I really enjoyed anybody that would do something different. When I was growing up, I remember, as far as music goes, I always loved Elvis Presley, because he created such a change for everybody. He made the adults all go crazy and say, "Well, no! You can't do this. You can't do that." But he kept on going and became very famous.

The other person that I always liked to read about was Eleanor Roosevelt. I think that Eleanor Roosevelt was absolutely one of the best first ladies that we ever had in this nation—specifically, because she cared about people, and she cared about their well-being. Even after her husband was no longer the president, after he passed away, she continued on with her work. And she did very groundbreaking work.

And, of course, I'm very partial to my grandmother, who was a Blackfeet woman. She was a daughter of Mountain Chief, one of the famous Blackfeet chiefs. He was the leader for the Blackfeet Nation. And they camped around a specific area, right down around Fort Benton. It was a long way from where the Blackfeet Nation is now. Blackfeet camped in clans, and when she was there by the Missouri River, where all the fur traders came up the river, she met my grandfather, who was full-blooded French. He had come from upstate New York and decided that he wanted to travel West. He stopped in Fort Benton at the Missouri River where all the boats stopped. And that's where my grandmother was camped. I guess they fell in love. Probably he had to give several horses, because she was the daughter of the chief, and that is what chiefs required—that you had to give.

She had to be an awfully brave woman to marry someone from out of her culture. And he spoke French, and she spoke Blackfeet. So she was very brave, and so she has always been one of the people that I admired. I always try to manage my life the way that I thought she would manage her life.

ROB: Did she and your grandfather end up bilingual?

ELOUISE COBELL: Yes. Their children definitely were bilingual. One of their parents spoke total French, and the other spoke total Blackfeet. My grandfather's name was Paulet Pepion, and he spoke total French. My grandmother's name was Little Snake Woman. They understood each other, so you know that they must have both learned to understand each other's language. They had ten children.

I always loved to read and listen about how the Blackfeet networked in with other regions and other races, because a lot of the people right now are not full-blooded Blackfeet. For instance, my father was half French and half Blackfeet, but we learned more about the Blackfeet culture than we've ever learned about the French culture. We don't know a lot about the French culture right now.

ROB: I know that you grew up very poor—you had no phone, electricity, or running water in your home. And that you went to a one-room schoolhouse. That's very different from the childhood that most people in this country enjoy. How do you think that beginning has changed you from what you might have been had you grown up with a comfortable income in your family?

ELOUISE COBELL: Wealth is measured differently. Although we didn't have the conveniences that other people have, and we didn't have the wealth that other people had, we had wealth in family. And family was so important to us. And so we really worked with each other and really gained a love for each other as a large family. I came from a large family. We lived out in the middle of the country. And so we were sort of interdependent on each other. We all had chores. Everybody had something to do. But we learned so much more about life and the landscapes that we were raised on. We enjoyed it, and because we didn't communicate with a lot of other communities, we didn't feel that we were a hardship family. We just felt that we were a very wealthy family, because we saw in the landscape, in the nature, and in our culture all the wealth that we had. And we didn't want a lot more.

ROB: What was the typical day like for you when you were about thirteen?

ELOUISE COBELL: When I was thirteen I was very busy. As I said, we had a lot of responsibilities as young people. Going back before I was thirteen, I always thought that every girl my age (in the second or third grade) had to walk straight home from school, walk into the kitchen, and start peeling potatoes. I never knew of anything different.

When I was thirteen, I was going into freshman year. We didn't have a high school in our particular area of the Blackfeet Nation, so we had to meet the bus about the same place where I attended the one-room country school. I rode the bus to an off-reservation school. It was very foreign to me at the beginning because there were probably just four Native students total. One was my brother, and two were my cousins. It was difficult getting adjusted to going to school with non-Indians. I had a very hard time. That's when I first noticed all of the material wealth that people had. Kids my age had a lot of material wealth compared to other students. But it was also a very exciting time of my life because I've always loved school.

I used to go to a one-room country school. When you went to a one-room school it was the first grade through the eighth grade. So you just took turns having classes, and the older children would help the younger students. And so that's how your education unfolded. So, to go into a high school where all of a sudden there were lockers, and there were bells that rang for you to change classes to another class, it was very different. It took a lot of adjustment. But I think that the eagerness and the energy to learn more just overrode some of those inhibitors.

ROB: I always thought that the Blackfoot and the Blackfeet were just different ways of spelling the same Indian tribe. But then I learned that they are actually two very different tribes and that yours, the Blackfeet, are related to the Sioux from the Dakota area. Is that right?

ELOUISE COBELL: We were actually called the Pegan tribe, the Real People tribe. The name Blackfeet came from the non-Indian settlers when they were moving West. They saw the bottoms of our moccasins, that were blackened, and so they called us the Blackfeet. We always make a joke and say, "If we had been wearing Reeboks, we'd have ended up the Reebok tribe!"

But we're really the Pegan tribe. We're the Southern Pegan tribe because we were the Blackfeet Confederacy made up of several tribes. The Blackfeet Confederacy is made up of the Southern Pegan (which we are because we're south of the United States' border) and then the Northern Pegan tribe up in Canada, and the Sitsiki, the Blackfeet up in Canada. Those tribes make up the Pegan Nation.

When the Blackfeet camped, they camped in bands. For example, I told you about the Mountain Chief band. OK, that was our band, and we were in the southern part of the Blackfeet Nation. So we camped here. And maybe the Heavy Runner band camped in this area, and another band camped up here, and one camped up here. And then when they came and did the imaginary border that split Canada and the United States, they didn't take into consideration that this was all our country. And so these particular bands in Canada became Canadian people, but we speak the same language. We have relatives that go back. The lineage goes back to the chiefs. We were supposed to be able to travel the border with ease, going back and forth. But now we're pretty much known as the Blackfeet Nation.

ROB: Do you speak Blackfeet?

ELOUISE COBELL: No, I don't. We have a total-immersion school now because there was an effort to wipe out our language that was done by the government and certain religions brought into our communities. They said we had to be civilized and we had to be assimilated into what everybody else looked like. So they wouldn't let us speak our language, and they wouldn't let us practice our religious beliefs. You were actually beaten for going against that. And so a lot of parents didn't want their children to be punished, and they wouldn't teach their children the Blackfeet language.

Now we're finally getting over that. And we've started language schools. And we've got the elders, who are the last speakers, to start teaching the young people.

ROB: I'm glad they finally stopped the beatings!

ELOUISE COBELL: It was hard for our ancestors. Our ancestors suffered a lot just to hang onto their culture. But you know, as a lot of the teachers will tell you, that we're stereotyped, like the article you read that said that we really don't need an accounting because we don't understand—we're noncompetent. And I think today was a really good example to show you that that is really not the case.

ROB: Were you taught, when you were my age, to make any of the traditional crafts?

ELOUISE COBELL: Oh yes. Our grandfather lived with us. We were pretty fortunate, and we all were taught the crafts. Unfortunately, my grandmother passed away when I was very, very young, but my grandfather used to make all kinds of different Indian objects. He would make different bows for my brother, and he would teach him how to go out and hunt with the bows. Of course we all learned about beading, although I am not a good beader. We really liked going to what some people called "powwows"—celebrations where you danced, and you learned.

We were taught when we were young, kind of in a hidden fashion, to really respect who we are, that we're Native Americans and we should be really proud of who we are. I was very happy that our parents taught that, even though they were punished. My father was punished when he was young because of speaking his language. And so he wouldn't teach us that. But when we would sit down to supper and all of our meals, we'd all call for everything in Blackfeet. We'd call for *nap-i-en*—that's bread. We called for different items on the table. We were never taught to speak it fluently just because they didn't want us to get into trouble. But now it's just wonderful because we're finally regaining our recognition, and we're no longer frightened of the government. That's the story. We're not frightened to make the government accountable for our money, too.

ROB: Who are your heroes now?

ELOUISE COBELL: I think my heroes have changed from the high-profile to the lower-profile people. A lot of my heroes are the ancestors that have really suffered and I see today who are still hanging on to their culture. Susie Whitecalf is one of my heroes. She is my neighbor, and has all these grandchildren, and she's raising them in the Blackfeet way. She continues to work.

My heroes are the minibank students from the Blackfeet Nation who are out there learning that they will always ask, "Why?" when there's something wrong with their money. That's what we're teaching them, that they will always ask, "Why?" They will not take, "We'll get back to you in two weeks or three weeks."

I think the people that have installed the language school that is now going to be teaching languages, they are my heroes.

I believe that my heroes have really changed, because I used to think about a non-Indian as a hero, because they were the only ones that could achieve that success. But now my heroes are changing to things that you're doing. You're picking out people that are lower profile, that are just making a difference. I think we learn that. You've certainly learned that a lot earlier in life. I think we learn that as we grow older. It's not the Madonnas [and] it's not the movie stars—the high-profile people—that really count.

I think there's so many people in our community, like I said, the young people that are implementing the financial literacy, so that we can ensure that the government is always accountable, that we never ever allow this to happen again.

ROB: I know that this quest to make the federal government accountable for the Indian trust money has taken over your life for the past several years. Once it's resolved, what are your next goals?

ELOUISE COBELL: I love working in the banking area, as you can tell. There are very few banks in Indian country. We at the Blackfeet National Bank were one of the first ever banks to be established in the heart of an Indian nation. So I had the opportunity to work with establishing a group of tribes uniting to create a Native American bank that would benefit many more Native Americans. I think that access for people, and not only native people but people of lower income, shouldn't be denied.

There's no wealth in our community. If you visit Indian nations you don't see a lot of wealth. Why is that? It's because the government has jumped in the middle and said, "You can't mortgage your land to build a home because it's trust. You can't do this. You can't do this." I would like to be there to change a lot of those laws that inhibit Native people from accessing the ability to build a home, to start a business in their community. Even though I've been instrumental in creating banks, I think that the work is not finished. We have to continue to break down barriers. We have to continue to really work with our people, to continue building our foundation. I feel—I don't know if people understand this—that we are almost like a third-world country, because we are sovereign nations. We have to understand how to build our economies and how important it is to really patronize each other in our businesses and not drive off the reservation and go to Billings, Montana, to do all our shopping. We've got to learn how to build right within our own nation so we make them very strong, and we make the people's pride very valuable again.

ROB: What do you do to relax?

ELOUISE COBELL: I like to visit family. I like to camp. A lot of my family comes home during the summer months. There is North American Indian Days that happens in Browning, Montana. It's a celebration where all the people camp and we attend that. But we have our own family encampment, and we're able to visit each other, and it's something that I really look forward to, just bringing family together. That relaxes me because what you do is you turn off everything that you've been working on. First of all, they get tired of listening to me on matters of the Indian trust funds, because I've talked about it for so long! We try to just talk about family things, introduce ourselves to new babies, new people that are getting married, and that's very relaxing to me, to interact with family. And we live on a small ranch, and so it's just fun to be out in the country and turn off the cities and the airplanes and just walk around and enjoy the nature, listen to the coyotes, listen to the birds. It's really fun to enjoy the landscape.

ROB: What are some of the traditional foods in your family?

ELOUISE COBELL: Berries. And of course buffalo. Because of this, my family would make pemmican [a food consisting of beef, dried fruit, and suet]. They'd take the berries and dry them, and they'd dry the meat, and then you mix them together. And they'd use fat from the buffalo and make the mixture round like bouillon cubes. And so when you'd travel you would just store them in your bags, and you just add them to boiling water, and then you have your soup. We were pretty much meat eaters. We're Plains Indians. We go into withdrawal if we don't eat meat.

ROB: Do you believe in God? Or do you follow the traditional religion of the Blackfeet?

ELOUISE COBELL: I believe in the creator. I don't see it any different than God—the creator that created us—the creator that created the mountains. I don't believe in structured religion. I believe in praying to the landscapes. I believe in praying to the mountains. I believe in thanking the creator for every single day that we live, and to have our lives and our grass and our landscapes, water, and trees. And that's what I believe.

Is it totally the way that my people believe? No, not to that extent. Is it totally in line with a structured religion viewpoint? No. I think that it's a combination that makes me feel comfortable.

ROB: Do you have any children?

ELOUISE COBELL: Yes. I have a son that turned thirty-two yesterday. He was raised on the same ranch where I was raised all my life.

He does very well. He went off to college and got his degree and is doing very well.

ROB: I appreciate your patience. That's all the questions I have. Thank you very much.

ELOUISE COBELL: Rob, I think it's really important that you're making a difference—that you're certainly a hero in taking on this project. Because what you're doing is you're going outside of your boundaries to learn about other people, and I think that's what amazed me when I read your letter. I read all of the letters that I received as a result of the *Parade* magazine article. And there were boxes full, and four thousand e-mails. And I read every single one of them. But yours jumped out at me because I thought your style of writing had a lot of empathy to what I was working on. You're the first one that I e-mailed back and said that I would like to do the interview, because I think you're a hero in your own right, just because you're interested. You don't have to be interested. You could live in your comfortable home in Salt Lake and say, "Well, that's another race. That doesn't have to do with me." But what I read through your letter was you said, "This has a lot to do with me because I'm an American citizen, and I will not tolerate the government's behavior of treating a certain race of people like this. So, I'm interested. And I like the fact that there is somebody out there fighting for that." So I think that when we look at it from that viewpoint, you're certainly one of my heroes.

ROB: I appreciate that.

ELOUISE COBELL: And that's exactly what I think.

8

Carroll Spinney

Because he is eight feet two inches tall when he's in costume, some people have called Carroll Edward Spinney the *biggest* star in children's television. For the past thirty-six years Spinney has played the character that he helped develop when "Sesame Street" first started on television on November 10, 1969. More than 148 countries have shown "Sesame Street." Carroll Spinney's character was named a "Living Legend" by the Library of Congress in 1990, and he has his own star on the Hollywood Walk of Fame. In spite of all this fame, Spinney walked right by me as we arrived at the television studio for our interview and I didn't recognize him. I bet almost nobody would recognize Spinney as he walks down the street. The reason is because the character he developed and plays is "Sesame Street"'s Big Bird. He also plays Oscar the Grouch.

Spinney was born in Waltham, Massachusetts, on December 26, 1933. From the time he was very young he wanted to work with puppets. Spinney was fascinated from the time that he saw his first puppet when he was five years old. When he was eight he bought his first puppet at a rummage sale. It was a monkey with a hole in its head, and Spinney paid a nickel for it. It didn't take him long to begin putting on puppet shows using his monkey puppet. He charged two cents for admission; his first show had sixteen people in the audience, and he thought he was a big success because thirty-two cents was enough money to get him into a movie theater.

After high school Spinney attended Boston's College of Art and Design in their Art Institute. He still enjoys creating fine art. He has some of his own paintings hanging in his office, and whenever Big Bird draws something on "Sesame Street," it is Spinney who has drawn that picture. When he was younger he drew a comic strip.

In 1955 Spinney made his television debut. Television was very new, and all the shows were produced live. He was paid ten dollars a week in Las Vegas to be part of the "Rascal Rabbit" show doing puppetry. Unfortunately, Spinney, who was in the air force at the time, was shipped out to Germany, and his gig on television ended.

It took five years, but after he was done with the air force Spinney returned to television work. This time he was part of the "Bozo the Clown" show. He did puppetry work on it and also played different side characters.

During a puppetry convention in Salt Lake City, Spinney gave a demonstration. Everything he tried to do went wrong in the performance. In spite of that, Jim Henson, the Muppet creator, approached Spinney afterward and told him that he liked what Carroll had tried to do. Henson was already a well-known puppeteer, so the praise meant a lot to Spinney. Henson invited Spinney to join him in New York; he said that he was creating some new puppets and wanted Spinney's help to do it. One puppet was going to be a grouchy character that lives in the gutter amid a lot of trash. The other was going to be a funny-looking and very tall bird.

Eventually Spinney moved to New York City. Henson's idea for Oscar the Grouch was that he would be orange, so that's how he was the first season. Big Bird was to be a pathetic-looking bird, and he was to have a yokel's accent. By the second season, Oscar had turned green, and Big Bird slowly changed into the character that the world knows today.

Spinney believes that Big Bird has a very important job, even though he looks kind of silly. He knows that there are millions of people all over the world who learned their letters and numbers from Big Bird when they were preschoolers. Big Bird has also taught millions of people memorable lessons about the importance of kindness.

Carroll Spinney sees Oscar's job as making children laugh. But Oscar reinforces Big Bird's counting lessons by counting his garbage with the television viewers.

The Big Bird puppet is two feet taller than Spinney is. Spinney's head ends in Big Bird's neck. He sees through holes in the neck, although he can't see very well. He has a small television viewer inside the costume that shows him what the audience will see, so he knows how to move. His right arm holds up Big Bird's head. He uses his fingers to control Big Bird's eyelids and mouth. The headpiece is heavy, though, and Spinney can hold it up for only eleven minutes at a time. Sometimes he has gone for twenty minutes, but that's very hard. Spinney says that his right arm is much more muscular than his left arm because it has been holding up the headpiece for thirty-six years.

Carroll Spinney's left hand operates Big Bird's left wing. There is a piece of fishing line tied onto the right wing, and Spinney can make that wing move a little by tugging on the line.

Big Bird is actually called a "walkabout," not a puppet. That is because Spinney walks around inside the costume. Oscar is a traditional puppet. When Oscar appears, Spinney is hiding inside or behind the trash can. Similar to other puppets, Spinney's hand goes into Oscar's head, and he controls Oscar's mouth, eyebrows, and eyes with his thumb and fingers. If Oscar were ever happy, Spinney would make Oscar's eyes widen. He doesn't have to do that very often.

When the script calls for it, Spinney can play both puppets at once. He does that by having an assistant operating Oscar while Spinney is inside Big Bird's costume. Sometimes he tapes Oscar's lines ahead of time, but he can also deliver both characters' lines from inside Big Bird.

Big Bird is covered with four thousand turkey feathers. They start out white, but each is dyed light yellow at the tip and a yellow orange color at the base and then applied to the costume individually. His legs are actually a pair of pants that is made of fleece dyed orange. The feet, with a pair of loafers inside that fit Spinney's feet, are already attached to the legs. When I interviewed Spinney the pants were hanging on the wall of his office, ready for him to pull on. They reminded me of those footed pajamas that babies wear. Big Bird wears slippers to keep the feet clean when he's not on camera. The costume shop provides Spinney with special ones; the ones I saw were green with floppy bunny ears. Although Big Bird still has the original head that was made thirty-six years ago, his eyes need to be repainted regularly.

Spinney pointed out to me that real birds have knees, and they bend in the opposite direction from ours. Jim Henson had originally planned that Big Bird's operator would wear the costume facing backward so that the knees would bend in the right direction. Carroll Spinney is grateful that he hasn't had to spend the past thirty-six years facing backward!

Oscar the Grouch, on the other hand, is actually made out of bath mats. Several white bath mats were sewn together to form Oscar, and then the whole thing was dyed green in a washing machine so the color wouldn't be perfectly solid. Oscar is still the original puppet that was created for the second season of "Sesame Street." Viewers were told that Oscar was green instead of the original orange because he had been on vacation in Swamp Muddy Muddy. He said that the air was so damp there that overnight it turned him green.

Oscar stays in his garbage can in front of 123 Sesame Street, but on a couple of occasions he has moved around. Both in live concert shows and in the 1985 movie *Follow That Bird*, Spinney used a specially built walkabout puppet of a garbage man that carried the trash can around.

Spinney is married and has three adult children. He has grand-children as well. When Spinney retires he doesn't want Big Bird and Oscar to have to retire, too. So Spinney is training puppeteer Matt Vogel so that he can perform the two characters when the time comes.

Like the other heroes I met, Spinney has received many awards. In 2004 he was presented the James Keller Award because "through the use of an entertainment giant (Big Bird) and a grouch (Oscar the Grouch), he has brought comfort and joy into countless living rooms." The award said that the work that Spinney has spent his life doing crosses racial and gender boundaries and shows the virtues of friendship, patience, and kindness. It said that he uses highly orig-inal educational tools to teach millions of children all over the world.

I agree with all the things that the James Keller Award mentioned. I think that Spinney's contributions to children's television and to puppetry are amazing. His lifelong role as an educator of children through the loving example of Big Bird and the edgy wisdom of Oscar truly makes him a hero. I am especially impressed that he has been willing to be so anonymous all during his career in order to accomplish this.

How Rob Got the Interview

I got some likely looking names and addresses from the credits that they sometimes show at the end of "Sesame Street." I wrote letters to all those places and people, and eventually I heard from someone at the Jim Henson Company. He was very helpful and set up the interview for me.

My mom and dad and I took a night flight from Salt Lake, which got into New York at six A.M.! Luckily, the hotel had a room ready at that early hour, and all three of us collapsed into beds to sleep until the alarm went off to go to the interview.

As a result of being sleep-deprived, my whole memory of that day and the interview is kind of hazy. It feels more like a dream I had than like a memory from real life.

We had directions on how to take the subway from our hotel in Manhattan to the "Sesame Street" studios in Astoria, New York, which is in Queens. But when we got off the subway, the streets seemed very confusing. Our being so sleepy may have had something to do with that also. It seemed as if every time we approached a corner, the street we were walking on had changed names. We got very lost and finally stopped in a deli to ask directions.

I said, "Could you please tell me how to get to the Kaufman Astoria television studios?" The Eastern European couple behind the counter didn't have any idea where it was. So then my mom asked, "Can you tell us how to get (how to get) to 'Sesame Street'?" Honestly, I don't think she meant to quote the song from the television show, but I thoroughly expected the deli couple to burst into song and dance as they replied. They didn't do that, but they did know where the show was taped and gave us directions.

The interview was held in Spinney's office. All during the interview a loudspeaker would come on and the announcer would say, "We need Elmo on the set. Elmo to the set," or something similar. It was exciting to be there.

At the end of the interview, Spinney invited us to see the studio. I loved that. It is actually very small. The different scenes—the steps of 123 Sesame Street where the characters often sit, the storefront of the fix-it shop, the grocery store, Oscar's trash can, Big Bird's nest—are located right next to each other, giving the impression of a street. But there is no extraneous building. Every single element is used. Somehow they give the impression of it being much bigger just by the way they do camera angles. To one side is a plain area with a blue screen behind it, where they do the filming for sequences that have the characters in front of imaginary sets.

While we were there, they were filming a segment with Elmo and some chickens and Gina the veterinarian. The puppeteers were sprawling on the floor, with their puppet arms straight up in the air.

It was up to the camera operator to make sure that he put the bottom of the picture above where you could see the puppeteers.

What I liked most about the studio is that the actors and puppeteers were having a lot of fun. They would improvise a little with their lines and laugh out loud. The technicians would join in laughing. All of them were really enjoying themselves. Maybe that is why "Sesame Street" continues to be so successful even after thirty-five years, because the people making it are enjoying themselves so much that the viewers are compelled to enjoy watching it.

Interview

KAUFMAN ASTORIA STUDIOS, ASTORIA, NEW YORK, DECEMBER 5, 2001

ROB: I know that you are a puppeteer, but I think of puppets as small things that fit over your hand and wrist. Your puppet is eight feet two inches tall. What is your definition of a puppet?

CARROLL SPINNEY: Well, Big Bird is certainly an exception. There are many, many forms of puppets. There are marionettes, which are also puppets. Of course they're often made of wood. Some puppets are quite simple. But Bird is sort of a clever invention of Jim Henson, where it's probably two-thirds costume and one-third puppet. It's a costume in the sense that you wear a good part of it. But rather than have the bird head on my head, instead I'm merely lost down inside the neck. And my hand is holding the bird's head up over my head.

ROB: Doesn't your arm get tired?

CARROLL SPINNEY: Oh yes. I guess it's just part of the puppetry business. We have a little saying about it: "If you're doing the puppets and you're comfortable, you're probably doing it wrong!"

ROB: Is your one arm much more muscular than the other?

CARROLL SPINNEY: It is, although it doesn't look any different. I've even heard stories, "Oh, his right arm is twice the size!" Well, they look exactly the same, but my right arm is definitely stronger. There's just no difference in size. It's just better toned, I guess.

ROB: It seems to me that your right wing moves.

CARROLL SPINNEY: It does move, thanks to that monofilament, which is fishing line. It shows once in a while—the light will glimmer on it. Of course, we don't like that to happen. That way when I move my left arm (because that's the only free arm I have left) it merely seesaws on the string. But at least that way it's not totally inert.

When we first started, the first few months, his right arm was pinned to his side, so that it looked like Big Bird had a broken wing. A couple of years ago there was a show called "Dudley the Dragon" on PBS. I remember someone said to us, "It's nice that they have this handicapped dragon (because his right arm was motionless)." I said, "No. They haven't discovered how to move the arm like we did." And sure enough, about a month later his right arm was moving. They had stolen our idea. That is how the "Bear in the Big Blue House" also works.

ROB: When you're in the Big Bird costume you work with a small wireless TV monitor strapped to your chest. What does it show?

CARROLL SPINNEY: I see the same picture that you see when you're watching the show on TV. That way I can see if Big Bird is looking at a character or looking into the camera. If I have to make a complex move, there are a couple of feathers attached with Velcro that I can move, so I can see out and look for a point of reference, like a door frame.

ROB: How did you get into puppets?

CARROLL SPINNEY: When I was eight, I bought a little puppet at a church rummage sale, and my mother gave me a stuffed flannel snake that she had made for me. For Christmas, she built me a Punch and Judy set. I thought using puppets was a great way to tell a story for kids. A puppeteer is a sort of a person who tries to be anything but himself.

ROB: You are known as Big Bird, yet you also do Oscar the Grouch. Which is your favorite? Each of them has such a distinct and well-rounded personality. How much have you been involved in the development of their personalities?

CARROLL SPINNEY: When Jim designed the puppets he gave me free rein as to how they'd act, although the scripts dictated a great deal. His image, though, of Big Bird was that he was a goofy guy. I said, "How should I play him?" He said, "Oh, you know, like Mickey Mouse's pal Goofy." He had seen me do a puppet show where I had a goofy dog named Pistachio. He talked like this, all weird, "How are you?" So that's how Big Bird sounded. If you notice, it sounds a great deal like Barney, "Hi. I'm Big Bird. Here I am." And it was really patterned after Mortimer Snerd, who was a funny, goofy hillbilly [hand puppet] who belonged to Edgar Bergen. It was big in the 1940s. I really preferred doing the Bird as a sweeter, nicer person.

On the other hand, Oscar is in the show very little lately. It's so much fun to play him. It's always good fun, I think, for actors to play villains. He's not a real villain, but he's certainly not pleasant. I've always said I wouldn't walk across the street to talk to a creep like him. But he is a lot of fun to play. I really enjoy him. But overall, I like the Bird best.

ROB: OK. How about their voices?

CARROLL SPINNEY: Well, the Bird evolved. When we first started, as I said, his voice was a bit Barney-ish (of course Barney didn't exist then). As the scripts came along I said, "You know, I think we shouldn't just be playing him as a big goofy guy. He should be a kid. So what if he's eight two? He's just a child." So that way he could be the surrogate child on the show—learning the alphabet, and what a square is, and all the other things. And Oscar's voice hasn't changed much at all. When I saw the puppets somehow I thought of Oscar's voice. I like it in that it's different from Big Bird's.

ROB: How did you learn to do different voices? And how many can you do?

CARROLL SPINNEY: Well, I started doing puppet shows when I was eight years old. I was doing voices all through my voice-changing period in adolescence. My mother was from England, so I started out with Punch and Judy. I had never actually seen a Punch and Judy show, so I had to make up the way it went. Eventually I had seventy puppets, and I tried to have each of them have a different voice. In reality, you only have about five or six voices that are very distinct. I'm not the world's greatest. I'm not like Mel Blanc (he was Bugs Bunny), who could do many many voices. That was his whole job. He didn't do puppets or anything. He just was a voice man. I would say that I only have a few voices. Maybe five.

ROB: As you know, my book is about heroes and what they were like when they were about my age. Who were your heroes when you were eleven to fourteen?

CARROLL SPINNEY: At eleven years old it was 1945 and the war was ending. My mother had said that it was the war to end all wars. I said, "Don't worry. There'll be another one when I'm old enough to be drafted." And sure enough, there was: the Korean War. My favorite things during those years were Disney films, and I particularly loved Charlie McCarthy. He was a very funny puppet on radio. He was very clever and very funny. I loved Jack Benny. There were lots of radio shows that I liked. They were the equivalent of sitcoms on TV, but were usually funnier, without a lot of the junk that they do now.

At fourteen I liked Western movies. I liked one character because he was tough and he didn't use a gun. If someone pulled a gun on him, he'd rip it right out of their hand with his whip. He always had a big bullwhip, so he didn't need a gun. It was ridiculous, but wonderful.

ROB: Do you think they would be happy with what you have accomplished?

CARROLL SPINNEY: I think so. I know that my mother, who started me with puppets at eight years old, was very proud. And last year the Library of Congress declared me a "Living Legend," which was humbling. So I've had an awful lot of acclaim. And I sometimes think it's really not fair. Some other people work very, very hard and dedicate their lives to very worthwhile things. There is education involved with what I do, but we try to be funny while we're educating. That's our hook. But we get more credit than some who are really unknown heroes. Not just firemen and stuff, but other people whose little inventions and things have made our lives so much healthier and better. So, in a lot of ways, I think the acclaim I get is not warranted. But it does make me feel very nice to have people say, "You're a hero."

ROB: I know that you were shy when you were my age. Did you read a lot? What were your favorite books?

CARROLL SPINNEY: I'm much more of a reader now than I was then. I have to confess that I was almost always on the honor roll, but I could have done a lot better. I could always manage to get homework done during the school day and would never take it home. I could have applied myself more. I could have done a lot better. I didn't read books. I always tended to read periodicals more than books, although I've read a lot of books.

My brother would read three books every two days! He was crippled. He had a mild form of cerebral palsy because of an injury at birth. It was an incredible malpractice situation. He was my older brother, and he was born at home. The doctor didn't want to leave a party. So he sent a midwife over who tied my mother's legs together. So for three hours his head pounded against the pelvis, wanting to be delivered. It damaged his brain enough to make it very difficult for him to walk. He only lived to be thirty-eight. I'd like a time machine to go back and speak to that doctor, or get there beforehand and make sure we had a *real* doctor. Or get her to a hospital, or something. But my brother was incredibly intelligent. And he was a wonderful artist. His hands were fine. He built all kinds of ships and things. I still miss him. I still cry.

I had another brother who was quite resentful of me coming along. He was a year and a half older. We only got to be friends a few years back. If you ever had any wise guys treat you hard at school—my brother always treated me that way until about two years ago. I love him now. We just don't talk politics. People in show business tend to be a little more liberal. He kind of feels like the Michigan militia is a little too far left for him!

I didn't quite finish that question. I sidetracked myself. Would you repeat it?

ROB: Did you read a lot of books?

CARROLL SPINNEY: I can't say that I really read a lot at that time. But I did read newsmagazines cover to cover, and I was always up on things. So I could carry my end of the conversation about current events or science. I've always been very interested in science and space. As a matter of fact, I was actually asked to go up in the *Challenger*. They asked me before they asked Christa McAuliffe. The astronauts wanted to bring more attention to their program. With kids, in particular, in America, how could you compare "Star Trek" with NASA? So they thought, if Big Bird went up, then people would pay attention. And indeed they would. But we found there was no room in the shuttle to put him in the capsule part. I was going to suggest, "Well, he could stay in outer space. Put him in the big bay with the door shut." They probably could have done that—just go through the lock when they need the costume, bring it in, warm it up. So, instead, Christa McAuliffe went, unfortunately. I'm very glad that Big Bird didn't go. But the idea of going to orbit Earth—that was the most incredible opportunity I could ever have!

ROB: What were your goals when you were about my age?

CARROLL SPINNEY: Well, I discovered puppets when I was eight, and I discovered art when I was six. I did that painting on the wall, for instance, but the original is much larger. That's a print. It is a drawing I did about twenty-two years ago. I was going to do a whole series about a planet that was completely overcome with vegetation. And I did quite a few pictures in that series. One of these days I'll just have to finish that series.

But by the time I was eight or ten I had decided to do what I'm doing now. When I was twelve, and TV had just started, in 1947, there was a puppet on it. There was obviously a man doing it. And it was so badly done! My puppets were better than his! He couldn't lip-sync. I said, "If *he's* on television . . ."—because anybody on television then was going to make a fortune. So I decided that I wanted to have a television show. It took a long time. I was thirty-five when I got this job, but I'd been in television since 1955. When I was twenty-one I had a show in Las Vegas for ten dollars a week. And then I got transferred to Germany with the air force, and that ended that. Then in 1960 I got back into television in Boston for ten years.

ROB: You've achieved wonderful success. You've earned four Emmys. The Library of Congress named you one of their Living Legends. Ten million kids see "Sesame Street"—of which your character is the anchor—each day, just in this country. It's seen in at least 148 countries. But, in spite of all this, you are an invisible celebrity. When you aren't in costume, no one would ever recognize you. I'll bet you don't get preferential treatment in restaurants. People don't ask you for an autograph.

CARROLL SPINNEY: That's true. I've been described as the most unknown famous person, which is very nice. I like that because fame is often more annoying than it is a pleasure. And I've gotten quite a few accolades, which seem to assuage my ego.

ROB: Tell me why you've been willing to give up your career for this one puppet.

CARROLL SPINNEY: Well, it's a fabulous career. I haven't given up anything. I've gained eventually. The pay was pathetic. I took a big pay cut from the "Bozo Show" in Boston to come here to "Sesame Street." There were a great many more expenses. I could drive in

Boston from my home (I still have that same home). We live in a tiny apartment here during the week when I'm working. But I'm doing exactly what I dreamed of doing. And to have all these children like something you do is very gratifying. Eventually I got paid more than the average person, except someone in Hollywood.

I married a secretary from "Sesame Street," and we've had one of the most perfectly happy marriages on earth for eight years. My wife is just an angel. We're exactly alike except she's a girl. So I have an awfully happy life.

ROB: Who are your heroes now?

CARROLL SPINNEY: I don't know how to answer that. Certainly the heroes of our recent grim events. I really enjoy certain sitcoms and things, but heroes—some scientists and great astronomers. I was a fan of Carl Sagan and the events in space that he revealed to us.

ROB: What would you like to be doing in five or ten years?

CARROLL SPINNEY: I'm enjoying writing. I'm writing a book about myself and Big Bird and Oscar. I'm going to become a lecturer. I have an agent for that. I'll be cutting back some more with "Sesame Street," but I hope to still be doing some of this. I plan to start selling art prints of my pictures for children. They all feature Big Bird—which I do not own. I have to get permissions.

ROB: Do you believe in God?

CARROLL SPINNEY: Yes. I don't understand much about it. And my belief is not quite as rigid as it used to be. I have a lot of strength in my thoughts and spiritual things. I really do think there is some form of afterlife. I've had a few remarkable experiences that can only say, "Somebody is there."

ROB: Noah Wyle, the actor, said that you are the most dedicated actor he knows. Jim Henson said that you are the only genius he has ever known.

CARROLL SPINNEY: I thought that about him! I don't think of myself as one. I must contact Noah Wyle. He said that? Because I worked with him just one day. It was just incredible. He is the same age as my son. My son draws as well as I, but he's a waiter. And he's thirty-one this next week. "Get off your duff!" [He laughs.] I made up my mind when I had children to love them and not eat my heart out if they don't do what I want.

ROB: Thank you for your time.

CARROLL SPINNEY: Oh, you're very welcome. I hope that was all right. I'm sorry I have to go. Oscar is back on. Would you like to stay and see any of the show? Do you want to see the studio?

ROB: Sure!

CARROLL SPINNEY: Great. Let me take you right in there.

9

Desmond Tutu

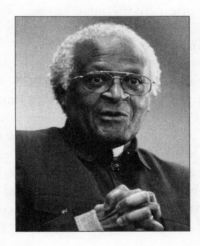

The Archbishop Desmond Tutu is a highly educated and an extremely spiritual man. He has used clear, expressive language to express his ideas on nonviolence and peace, and he has become a figure of peace in South Africa and in the world.

Desmond Mpilo Tutu was born at Klerksdorp, South Africa, on October 7, 1931. Klerksdorp is about 120 miles from Johannesburg, the richest city in the country of South Africa. Tutu's family, in common with all the other black people in South Africa, had very little money. The Tutu family lived without running water or electricity in a small shack even though his father was a respected schoolteacher.

At that time in South Africa, the black people had to always carry passbooks and special identification with them, even though they formed the majority of the population. The white police would sometimes stop a black person on the street and demand to see his or her papers.

When Desmond Tutu was fourteen he caught tuberculosis and almost died. He was stuck in a bed in a hospital, away from his family and among men who were dying, for almost two years. During that time a white priest from England named Trevor Huddleston came to talk to him every day; he was a very influential person in Desmond Tutu's life.

In 1948 an election was held in the country of South Africa. Only white South African citizens were allowed to vote. The National Party, which was openly racist, was elected to lead the country. The new leaders called for apartheid, which means "apart-hood," and they promised to introduce government policies that were against the black people. It was during this time that Desmond Tutu married Leah Nomalizo, and they eventually had four children. Tutu was one of only a few black people who were allowed to enter a university. He had always dreamed of becoming a doctor, but his family couldn't afford all that schooling, and so he became a teacher like his father was.

In 1955 the racist South African government introduced a new education law called the Bantu Education Act. It was designed to make sure that black children would receive an inferior education. The law said exactly what could be taught in black schools, and it didn't include much math or science. The government was deliberately trying to keep the black people uneducated. Desmond Tutu decided that he couldn't be a teacher under the Bantu Education Act. He believed that black children should be able to get as good an education as the white children received. So he left teaching and entered a theological college to become an Anglican priest.

Eventually the Tutu family left South Africa so that Desmond Tutu could study theology at King's College, in London, England. He also worked there as an assistant curate. While they lived in London, Tutu discovered a whole new world as far as race relations were concerned. People of every color were treated the same. Sometimes Desmond Tutu would ask a policeman in the street for directions. He would do it just for the pleasure of hearing the policeman address him as "sir" and answer him in a respectful way.

Soon afterward, Tutu returned to South Africa, to the city of Lesotho. He began lecturing there and in the country of Swaziland. He became well known in the Anglican Church and had the opportunity to travel to many poor countries in Africa for the church. In 1975 Tutu was elected Dean of Johannesburg for the Anglican Church. He was the first black person to ever hold that position. Once he was in such a visible position, every speech he gave was heard and quoted all over the world.

By 1979 Tutu had joined with some other black leaders in calling for international sanctions against South Africa. That means that other countries would formally and publicly condemn the South African policy of apartheid. Eventually the United States and other countries stopped trading with South Africa, and so there were economic sanctions as well. Other sanctions sometimes used are diplomatic or cultural, or they involve armed forces. Tutu believed this was the only way to protest without using violence, and he was very afraid that there would be a bloodbath in South Africa if things didn't change.

On October 15, 1984, Desmond Tutu was awarded the Nobel Peace Prize. It was seen as a sign of support for the black people in South Africa who were trying to change apartheid without violence. The award recognized the importance of human dignity and democracy in South Africa. It was awarded to Tutu because of his leadership in helping people develop the courage and heroism that the black population had shown in their use of peaceful methods of fighting against apartheid. In his acceptance speech Tutu called for peace, love, and brotherhood of all people. Tutu established the Southern African Refugee Scholarship Fund and used his Nobel Peace Prize Fund to help disadvantaged students further their studies.

Desmond Tutu was elected the Archbishop of Cape Town in 1986. It is the highest position in the Anglican Church in South Africa. He was the first black person to ever be named archbishop. Whites and blacks both attended the enthronement ceremony, but the government would not allow all of the many international dignitaries who were invited to enter the country.

Apartheid finally ended in South Africa in 1994. There was a free election, and Nelson Mandela was elected president. Archbishop Tutu has stated that he believes one of the reasons for their success, with so little bloodshed, is that no other country in the world has been prayed for as much as South Africa was during apartheid. I was only six years old in 1994, but I remember prayers in our family where one of my parents would ask God to help end apartheid.

After retiring as archbishop in 1996, Desmond Tutu became the chairperson of the Truth and Reconciliation Commission in South Africa. The commission's purpose was to investigate and collect testimony about human rights violations and other political crimes that happened between 1960 and 1994. Then the commission would consider granting amnesty for those people who confessed about their participation in the crimes. Amnesty is a pardon granted by a government, especially for political offenses. It means that the individual might not be punished, even for atrocities, if they publicly confess them. Archbishop Tutu hoped that if he "opened wounds to cleanse them, they wouldn't fester." He believed that you couldn't forgive things that you don't know about. During a two-year period, twenty-one thousand victims came to the commission to tell their stories.

Desmond Tutu believes that there was a lot of healing that happened during this time, just because people were able to share their stories. The commission brought together victims and persecutors from the apartheid era. Many of the victims forgave their oppressors. The goal of Archbishop Tutu and the other members of the commission was to try and balance the requirements of peace and reconciliation with justice and accountability.

I guess it's pretty obvious why I consider Archbishop Tutu such a hero. I hope that I never find myself in circumstances similar to those in South Africa in the second half of the twentieth century. But if I do, I hope that I have the courage and the faith in the goodness of people that Desmond Tutu has. I have the impression that he might be a shy person. He certainly didn't ask for the job of being spokesperson for the antiapartheid forces. But he found himself there, and he went forward with dignity and humor and infinite courage.

How Rob Got the Interview

When my brother Will first started this heroes project, Nelson Mandela and Desmond Tutu were both on his list of heroes. Mom told Will that there was no way that we could travel to South Africa so Will could conduct an interview. So both of these men went into the "wish list" of people that we knew were real heroes but felt there was no way we could connect with them.

Then in the winter of 2002 the Olympics came to Salt Lake City, Utah, where we live. Suddenly Salt Lake was a much more consequential city than it had been before. My parents read in the newspaper that Archbishop Desmond Tutu was going to be in town to participate in a panel discussion.

Immediately we started scheming to figure out who we knew that might be connected to the event. We finally came up with a neighbor who knew someone who knew someone who might have a connection with the event. So I wrote a letter to my neighbor, enclosed a letter to the archbishop, delivered the letters to my neighbor, explained what I was doing, and asked her to pass along the letter to Tutu.

In one of those nice coincidences that sometimes happen, my neighbor mentioned my project to her daughter who is a reporter for one of the Salt Lake City newspapers. Amazingly, her daughter had a meeting scheduled with the Reebok people the very next day. And it turned out that Reebok was the company sponsoring Archbishop Tutu's appearance at the event. The Reebok people liked my project, and somehow the CEO of Reebok, Paul Fireman, heard about me. The next day someone from Reebok called to say that I was invited to their Humanitarian Awards Presentation, at which Desmond Tutu was the guest speaker, and that they had arranged interview time afterward for reporters, including me, to meet the archbishop.

The day of the Reebok presentation started with a frantic drive trying to get from our house to the Capitol Theatre downtown. It was the day before the opening ceremony for the Olympics. With all the roadblocks for the Olympic torch run I was starting to feel like a mouse in a maze. But finally we got there.

As soon as I stepped inside, I walked up to the media desk, and they asked me if I was Robert Hatch. I, of course, said yes, and they handed me a pass that said PRESS on it. One of the Reebok employees escorted me to the press section, which was right at the very front of the auditorium. There were journalists there from the local newspapers as well as the BBC, *The New York Times*, *USA Today*, *Extra*, and many others.

The award ceremony itself was really elaborate. They had brought in national performing groups as well as one from Kenya. The celebrities presented the awards to the recipients. Finally it was Desmond Tutu's turn in the program. He had a strong sense of humor, and he made a couple of jokes. He had the whole audience recite with him that "we are very special people." He looked like a frail yet competent man, and he looked experienced, as if he'd seen quite a few things. He had sparkling eyes, like those you might picture on Santa Claus. During the finale everyone from the cast was on the stage dancing and singing. He joined, gently, in the dance, and he was grinning. He looked as if he was enjoying himself.

Afterward there was a spot set up backstage for the press. Maybe forty journalists were crowded around, with all sizes and types of cameras. There were very hot lights trained on the archbishop. For several minutes he patiently posed for photos. It was really hot even where I was standing. I don't know how he stood it right in front of all the lights.

Finally it was my turn to interview Archbishop Tutu. As soon as I started it became obvious that the archbishop had no idea who I was or why he was faced with a kid wanting to interview him. I tried to explain my project to him. One of the official Reebok people who was standing there cut in to say that I had only five minutes to do my interview. I was very nervous. My mom was also nervous and couldn't make the tape recorder work. After about five questions the Reebok guy cut me off and showed us out.

Because I hadn't finished the interview, I decided to try and get a letter to the archbishop while he was still in town, asking if I could please have a few more minutes to finish the interview. I wrote letters and sent them to all the best hotels in town, thinking that he must be staying in one of them. It was a great surprise to see Archbishop Tutu on the television the next night as one of the eight people who carried the Olympic flag into the opening ceremonies. But it didn't get me any closer to finishing the interview.

Then, a couple of weeks after the Olympics were over, there was an article in the religious section of the newspaper about Desmond Tutu and the local Episcopalian bishop with whom he had stayed while in Salt Lake. Eureka! So I wrote a letter to Bishop Sandra Tanner, the local Episcopalian bishop, and asked her if she would please forward my enclosed letter to Archbishop Tutu.

The Olympics were in February. In May, I received an e-mail from the archbishop's secretary, suggesting that we finish the interview via e-mail. So that is what we did.

Interview

THE REEBOK HUMANITARIAN AWARDS, CAPITOL THEATER,
SALT LAKE CITY, UTAH, FEBRUARY 7, 2002

ROB: Thank you very much for taking the time to talk to me. As you might know, my book is about my heroes and what their lives were about when they were my age. I'm thirteen. What books did you enjoy reading when you were about thirteen?

DESMOND TUTU: I'm seventy years old! It's hard to remember. *Lamb's Tales of Shakespeare. A Tale of Two Cities, Oliver Twist*, or anything by Charles Dickens. When I was older, the Bible and A. E.

Taylor's *The Faith of a Moralist*, and the work of Martin Luther King Jr.

ROB: How about over the course of your life? What is one book, one film, one play, one poem, and one piece of music that you would most like everyone to see, read, or hear?

DESMOND TUTU: Film—*The Mission* directed by Roland Joffe; book—Father Trevor Huddleston's *Naught for Your Comfort*; play—Shakespeare's *King Lear*; poem—"A man is a man for all that," by Robert Burns; piece of music—Handel's *Messiah*, a tremendous work.

ROB: Who were your heroes when you were about my age?

DESMOND TUTU: Have you ever heard of the "Brown Bomber"? He was Joe Louis. Fats Waller, Nat King Cole, Lena Horne. In my country we were told that we could not achieve anything. It was so exciting to see these people who were accomplishing things! I admired many U.S. African-American athletes, one baseball player—Jackie Robinson, even though I didn't know baseball. Boxers—Joe Louis, Sugar Ray Robinson, etc. Film stars—Lena Horne, Fats Waller, Cab Calloway, Louis Armstrong; we named our son after him and Trevor Huddleston.

I especially felt that Jesse Owens was a hero. He was a black sprinter who took the gold medal in the 1936 Berlin Olympics, despite that country's preference for white, Aryan youth. I love the way he disappointed Hitler!

My mother, though largely uneducated, was incredibly compassionate and concerned for the underdog, even though she herself was a double underdog, as a black and a woman. She had a big heart.

Have you heard of Trevor Huddleston?

ROB: Yes, I have read about him. [He's the white Anglican British priest who befriended Desmond Tutu while Tutu was hospitalized for more than a year.]

DESMOND TUTU: He was my hero. He was a deeply prayerful person, concerned for the marginalized poor and discarded. The voice of the voiceless—how courageous he has been.

ROB: What event during your lifetime has had the greatest effect on your political beliefs?

DESMOND TUTU: The death of Steve Biko. [He was the founder of the Black Consciousness movement in South Africa and died from brain injuries suffered during interrogation in prison in 1977.] It showed the heartless iniquity of apartheid, which would stop at nothing. It also gave us the callous remark from cabinet minister Jimmy Kruger, who said Steve's death "leaves me cold."

Meeting a hungry child at apartheid's dumping ground—the resettlement camps—who said when they had no food, "We fill our stomachs with water."

ROB: Which political figure—living or dead—do you most admire?

DESMOND TUTU: Julius Nyerere [formerly president of Tanzania]—human, wonderfully idealistic, and highly principled. Also a devout Catholic.

ROB: If you could visit any time in history for twenty-four hours, which would you choose?

DESMOND TUTU: I would like to have been in the physical presence of our Lord to discover the power he had over people for their good, enabling them to blossom as he made them believe in themselves as he believed in them.

ROB: What do you consider the greatest threat, at present, to individual freedom and liberty?

DESMOND TUTU: The hostility toward diversity. It leads to fundamentalism, authoritarianism, and ethnic cleansing, all because people are scared of difference.

ROB: On another important matter, whose opinion—other than your own—do you trust most?

DESMOND TUTU: Leah, my wife's. I couldn't survive otherwise.

ROB: If you could pass one law, what would it be?

DESMOND TUTU: To get rid of humbug and make us laugh at ourselves and not take ourselves so seriously. Having a sense of humor helped us to survive apartheid.

ROB: I know that your family spoke the Sotho language at home, but at age seven you started going to a British Christian school that was taught in English. Did you know any English before you started going there? How long did it take before you felt like you understood everything that was going on in English?

DESMOND TUTU: My home language was in fact Xhosa. I knew some English, very rudimentary before I went to school. It took a v-e-r-y l-o-n-g time!

ROB: I know that you know some Afrikaans, and that you can preach in Zulu. Do you speak any other languages?

DESMOND TUTU: I know Sotho, Tswana, Zulu, and of course Xhosa, English, and Afrikaans. I know a little biblical Greek.

ROB: You have spent much of your life communicating in English. What language do you dream in?

DESMOND TUTU: My dreams are polyglot!

ROB: You are pretty short—just five three—and I know that you were thin and frail when you were my age. Did the other kids tease you about that? If they did, how did you deal with it?

DESMOND TUTU: Actually not too much, though I was tweaked a bit. Once someone called me "Dove" disparagingly. Maybe they were being prophetic, a dove of peace.

I tried to build up my body, and perhaps because I was a bit clever they grudgingly respected me. I was not too much of a dud playing street soccer, and that helped me to survive taunts.

ROB: You have survived some awful illnesses, starting with when you were just a baby and your dad thought you had died—then when you were fourteen, and got tuberculosis and were hospitalized for twenty months! And it was a long train ride from where your family lived, so they probably couldn't visit very often. When I've got strep throat or something, about the fourth day I start going crazy, because I'm so bored and anxious to be better already. How did you get through all those lonely, boring months?

DESMOND TUTU: We were quite supportive of one another in the hospital. There were some American women missionaries who used to come to take church services and to distribute candy. I don't have to tell you which of their activities was the more popular. My mother was very regular in visiting at least once a fortnight. She was a great woman. I look like her and hope I resemble her spirit, too.

ROB: I know that Huddleston has said that your sense of humor helped you a lot. Did you play pranks or jokes on the other kids? Can you remember any of them?

DESMOND TUTU: We played a lot of draughts, which is a lot like checkers, and card games, because we were not allowed to engage in too much physical exertion.

ROB: At what point did you discover your belief in God? Was it already there when you were my age?

DESMOND TUTU: I came from a Christian home, and so it was something you took in with your mother's milk, as it were. But I was quite seriously ill and was coughing up blood. I had seen that most of the other patients who coughed up blood were carried out on a stretcher to the morgue. One day I went to the restroom as I coughed up blood and said to God, "If I must die, then, well, it's OK. If not, that's OK, too." I experienced a great sense of calm. I was just at the beginning of a long journey, which is still continuing today.

ROB: I know that the book containing all the laws defining apartheid was so big that it weighed five pounds. When did you first start to think that maybe you could play a part in changing that?

DESMOND TUTU: I never thought I would be involved in changing apartheid. It was other more capable and gifted persons who would do that—our leaders.

ROB: You wanted to be a doctor but became a teacher when your family couldn't afford to send you to medical school. Then, when you were twenty-five, the Afrikaans government basically tore apart the school system for blacks, and you quit teaching rather than teach what they would now permit. I know that you then trained to become a minister. I like what you've said, that it was like being "grabbed by God by the scruff of the neck in order to spread His word, whether it is convenient or not." Has it mostly been "inconvenient"?

DESMOND TUTU: It was quite rough in the struggle, but others suffered a great deal more than I did, or my family. We were harassed but not imprisoned for twenty-seven years, or detained without trial, or placed under house arrest as others were.

And I was able now and again to travel and to experience the marvelous support we had from the international community.

When the South African government took away my passport, Sunday school kids from St. James Church on Madison Avenue, in New York City, drew pictures and sent them as their passports of love! Wonderful! There were marvelous compensations. It was almost nice to be in trouble with the South African government, because it won us so much international support and confirmed our credibility.

ROB: I've read that you have an older and a younger sister. Your dad was tall and strict. He was a headmaster of a school, and your mom was short and very compassionate. What do you remember best about your family?

DESMOND TUTU: We were just an ordinary family with many friends in the community. It is extraordinary to think we could live reasonably normal lives in such an abnormal society.

ROB: I know that even you have spent at least one night in jail, that you once waded into an angry crowd of people who were trying to light a person on fire whom they thought was a police spy. Have you ever been afraid for your safety?

DESMOND TUTU: Oh, yes. I have been scared. But I have said to God, "If I'm doing your work, then you jolly well will have to look after me." Of course, for the Christian, death is not the worst thing that can happen, since Jesus rose from the dead and destroyed death thereby.

ROB: My questions have mostly dealt with the time when you were my age, and so I haven't asked you much about the extraordinary things that you have accomplished in your adult life. Are you pleased with what you have accomplished?

DESMOND TUTU: I have been greatly blessed to see the liberation of our people, to have the honor of introducing Nelson Mandela, as our newly elected president of a free and democratic South Africa, to South Africa and the world. I would have been contented to die thereafter. And then to have the incredible privilege of presiding over the process of healing a traumatized people in the Truth and Reconciliation Council is the cherry on the treetop. I have been blessed beyond my wildest dreams.

ROB: What more are you hoping to do?

DESMOND TUTU: I hope I can help us in the world to know that we are family.

ROB: Thank you so incredibly much for taking your precious time to answer my questions. I believe that not just me but a lot of kids will read your answers and gain insight, and maybe even courage, from them. Thank you again.

DESMOND TUTU: God bless you richly. Reach for the stars, since the sky is the limit.

10

Lance Armstrong and Linda Kelly Armstrong

Lance Armstrong is one of the all-time best athletes. Thousands of people in the United States became Tour de France enthusiasts when Armstrong won it the first time and have watched it almost fanatically ever since. Armstrong survived a deadly case of cancer before his first Tour de France victory. In spite of that, he has gone on to win seven consecutive victories, which no one else has ever done.

Lance Armstrong was born September 18, 1971, in Plano, Texas. He is the only child of a single mother, Linda Kelly Armstrong, who encouraged him to be involved in all kinds of sports. He had a natural athleticism and was very disciplined and focused where sports competitions were concerned. When he was thirteen he took second place in the Iron Kids Triathlon, a rigorous race that has three different parts: swimming, running, and biking. By the time he was sixteen he was a professional triathlete. Eventually he concentrated just on bicycle racing.

Aerobic conditioning is a term used to describe the relationship between a person's body weight and the maximum amount of oxygen that he or she can inhale and use. The Cooper Institute, in Dallas, studies the relationship in people between fitness and aerobic conditioning. When Lance Armstrong was sixteen, the Cooper Institute invited him to come to Dallas to be tested. In each of our bodies the oxygen we breathe is used to break down the food we eat and turn it into energy. If you can use more oxygen then you will have more energy and be better at whatever sport you choose. At the institute they gave Armstrong the VO_2 max test to measure his aerobic conditioning. Armstrong's score was higher than any test they had performed before. Now, as an adult, his VO_2 max score is about eighty-five milliliters per kilogram of body weight. That is more than twice the level of a healthy average-sized man.

Not only his lungs but also Armstrong's entire body seems to be especially designed for biking. His heart, for example, is one-third larger than average. It beats very slowly at rest—about thirty-two beats per minute. That rate is so slow that if a doctor didn't realize his level of athleticism and listened to Armstrong's heart, the doctor would probably immediately hospitalize him. When he is racing, Armstrong's heart can beat more than two hundred beats per minute. This wide range of heartbeat works to his advantage in racing. Also, his thighbones are extra long; this gives him added torque when he pedals. And Armstrong's body fat is unusually low. At the beginning of the 2004 Tour de France, it was around 5 percent.

Armstrong almost didn't graduate from high school with his class because he was training so hard. He ended up taking private classes to catch up on the work he had missed while training. His goal was to be able to train with the U.S. Olympic developmental team in Colorado Springs, Colorado. In the end he was invited to train there.

That summer Armstrong qualified for the 1989 junior world championships in Moscow. He kept working hard, and two years later he was the U.S. National Amateur Champion. He kept the amateur status through the Barcelona Olympics in 1992, where he finished in fourteenth place.

When Lance Armstrong was just twenty-one years old he won the 1993 one-million-dollar Thrift Drug Triple Crown. Then that same year he won the world cycling championship. He had become famous in the bicycling world. He went on to win the Tour Du Pont in 1995 and was named the American Male Cyclist of the Year by *VeloNews*. Armstrong decided that he was ready to begin giving back to his community in some way, and that year he established the Lance Armstrong Junior Olympic Race Series. He hoped that it would promote bike racing among young people in America.

Nineteen ninety-six started out as a great year for Armstrong. He had a new home near Austin and a beautiful Porsche to drive. He was the number one–ranked cyclist in the world and had signed a contract with the French Cofidis racing team that would earn him more than two million dollars over a two-year period. He was training for six to eight hours a day, and when he had pain and swelling in his groin, in didn't worry him. He didn't bother to have it checked by a doctor until he began to cough up blood and get headaches five months later.

The doctors found testicular cancer, which had spread to his brain and lungs. He had twelve golf ball–sized tumors in his lungs and lesions, or areas that had lost their function, in his brain. He was only twenty-five years old.

Lance Armstrong's chances of surviving the cancer were fifty-fifty, but he was determined to beat it and started a very aggressive form of chemotherapy.

Within a few months of his diagnosis, Armstrong started the Lance Armstrong Foundation. This is a nonprofit foundation that raises money for cancer research and helps to raise awareness of cancer. The foundation has raised millions of dollars.

Two years later Armstrong announced that the cancer was gone and he was ready to return to racing. Unfortunately, many people, including the Cofidis team, were skeptical. They didn't believe that he would have the strength and stamina to succeed in bicycle racing. The Cofidis people had actually ended his two million dollar contract when they heard of his diagnosis, and they were not interested in having him back.

Armstrong found a new team to join, the U.S. Postal Team, and they began preparations for the Tour de France.

The Tour de France is a grueling bicycle race. It has twenty different "stages," each of which is its own race, and covers more than two thousand miles through France, Luxembourg, and Germany, including steep mountain terrain. It has been estimated that a racer will burn up 5,200 calories a day during the twenty-one-day race.

Armstrong now says that cancer was the best thing that ever happened to him. He explains that he was such a good cyclist before that he didn't bother about teamwork or strategies. After the cancer he had added discipline and focus, and he worked well with the other team members. Everyone knows that the U.S. Postal Team won the 1998 Tour de France, and the next five as well. The race always ends in Paris, on the famous Champs Elysées, where crowds line the street. In 2004 those crowds saw Armstrong wearing the traditional yellow jersey that the race leader wears, wearing a golden bike helmet, and riding on a twenty-four-carat gold-leaf bike!

Armstrong has a son, Luke David, and twin daughters, Isabelle and Grace, with his former wife, Kristin Richard Armstrong.

What makes Lance Armstrong a hero for me is that while he seems to be totally infallible, he is fallible. He has to face doubt and challenges just as everyone else does. He has had failures in his life, but he is determined to win. Everything that he has, he has earned himself. He just never quits. He just seems to move on to even bigger challenges.

How Rob Got the Interview

As I read Armstrong's book *It's Not About the Bike*, I noted names of people who had been influential in his life. I had about thirty of these names and sent letters to each one of them asking for their help in contacting Armstrong. I tried to go through his agent; I tried to contact a member of his racing team who is from Utah. But I had no success. Finally I contacted his charitable foundation and was able to speak to someone there. She told me that Armstrong was training in Europe but would be in Austin, Texas, for forty-eight hours during his annual Ride for the Roses, raising money for the Lance Armstrong Foundation. (He raised three million dollars that weekend!) She was doubtful that he would have time to talk with me. We finally arranged for me to interview Linda Kelly Armstrong, Lance's mom, and have just a few questions for Armstrong himself. So that's what we did.

This was a fun interview, because Will accompanied me. It's the only one that we both worked on together. We met Linda Kelly Armstrong and Lance Armstrong in Austin.

The first thing that struck me about Armstrong was his boundless energy. This guy literally raced into a parking lot, ran inside, gave this great and powerful speech, answered a few questions, and raced back out to his truck and out of the parking lot. *Direction. Energy. Drive.* These were a few words this man personified. As a matter of fact, a couple of hours into the bike race, a car pulled up alongside Armstrong, and he climbed into it from his bike while it was still moving and was on his way to the airport! Unbelievable! It was really fun to see his mom, too, and see the same drive and determination in her. It's easy to see where he inherited many of his amazing traits from.

Will and I spent the weekend observing Armstrong from the sidelines. We had secured press credentials, because of the interview that was set up, and so we were able to watch him during the actual bike ride while we were riding in the back of a news truck that was full of journalists. It was driving right in front of the bikers. It was very cool. Sometimes he just coasted along. He made the race seem effortless. He was very gentle in the way he rode along with children and older folks, and then he would speed up to give the race leaders a little competition. Everybody was included, and it was incredible to watch the awe on people's faces as they pedaled along with the fastest biker in the world.

We don't often see great athletes who are willing to spend so much of their time and energy on things like raising money for cancer research. It was a privilege to see Lance Armstrong at close range and in full control.

———◆———

Interview

AUSTIN, TEXAS, APRIL 14, 2002

ROB: Who were Lance's heroes when he was about my age—eleven to fourteen?

LINDA KELLY ARMSTRONG: I think at that time Lance was doing a lot of cycling and triathlons and everything. So, I look back at that time and, believe it or not, Laurent Fignon was winning the Tour de France. Lance and I were watching it on television when Greg LeMond overcame a fifty-second deficit in the final time trial to win the Tour de France over Fignon by eight seconds (the smallest margin in history). And I remember sitting down and watching him finish that race, Lance and I both in front of the TV. And we just thought that was the neatest thing.

And then I would also say, because he was in triathlons, it was Mark Allen. You've seen pictures of him with Mark Allen.

ROB: Do you think they'd be proud of what he's accomplished?

LINDA KELLY ARMSTRONG: I know they'd be proud of what he's accomplished. It was funny, because back then he was the new kid on the block. And he was much younger than they were. Here he was, coming in second or third, placing in the top ten. And they were all looking around, "Who is this kid?" I think at the time, they said, "We're going to watch out for him because he's going places." To think that he got to this level is probably something none of us envisioned. I think they'd be really proud.

ROB: I know that Lance was a pretty angry person when he was my age. It sounds like you were kind of his best friend. I know how that feels. I feel kind of out of touch with kids my age. Mainly, I just bury myself in books when I get angry. But it seemed to me that when he got angry he just did a lot of bicycle riding. Do you think his anger, and his need to prove himself, is part of what made him a champion?

LINDA KELLY ARMSTRONG: I probably wouldn't call it anger as much as I would say that he had a lot of energy. From a very, very small age he had a lot of energy. And with that you can take it and channel it in a very positive way. Lance found an interest in running. As a parent, what I did was channel that energy and found something that he enjoyed doing. It wasn't pushing him into anything. But with anything like that you have to look at the positive and try to help him get there. He continued to exercise and train quite a bit.

ROB: He's in good shape now, with three gorgeous kids; he's a Tour de France winner and a national hero. Do you think it will be harder for him to push himself hard enough to win again?

LINDA KELLY ARMSTRONG: I think that the level of his athletic ability now is like any top athlete. They love the thrill of winning. It's all about the win. It's like getting out there and you've got to win. It's the only thing in their vocabulary.

ROB: Losing is not in their vocabulary?

LINDA KELLY ARMSTRONG: No.

ROB: What do you remember about Lance when he was my age?

LINDA KELLY ARMSTRONG: We had some of our very very best times together. Lance was funny. He was really funny. I like to say that he was a whole lot like Will Smith in "Fresh Prince." He could do a great impersonation of Will Smith. When he was your age there was a lot of structure. He was very good at calling me once he got home from school, and I would be working. Then he'd head out for a bike ride. "Mom, I'm going out for a fifty-mile ride. I'll be home at so-and-so time. What's for dinner?"

And it was a very structured environment, to a degree. He still had that other side to him. It wasn't all training. He still had that crazy side of him.

ROB: What did he like to read?

LINDA KELLY ARMSTRONG: That's a good question. Lance was a lot like me. It's very hard for us to sit down and focus on a book. But what he did read, and what we always did, was read the newspaper. And so he was always up on current events. To this day, that's the first thing we do is get the newspaper out. Everything's gone to the Internet now, but he could talk about current events, whereas most people his age weren't even reading the newspaper. Books were not his thing.

ROB: What type of music did he enjoy listening to?

LINDA KELLY ARMSTRONG: My goodness. Heavy metal. I remember taking him and all the boys to the Van Halen concert. I was the mom who rounded up the boys.

He loved heavy metal stuff. And I would come home from work and that stuff would be blasting. We had a small home. And I'd say, "Oh, son. I've had a hard day." And he'd say, "Mom, this is for you," and he'd put on Kenny G. He was so into pleasing me. It was so sweet. But he definitely loved his heavy metal.

ROB: What were his hopes and dreams when he was my age?

LINDA KELLY ARMSTRONG: I would say that at the time, your age, you start talking about what type of education you want to pursue and what major you want to talk about. I was always saying computer science. At the time that was a great degree to get. And then UT [University of Texas]. He's always been a fan of UT. And so I would say that he was at that time thinking of going to college and getting his degree in computer science.

ROB: Did you ever try to talk him out of bicycling?

LINDA KELLY ARMSTRONG: No. He was very bright in school, but academics were just not his thing. He was showing that he had tremendous talent in competition with cycling and other sports. So his senior year, and they're all going off to college, I said, "Son, you have two choices. You can try to secure a sponsorship and ride for a team, or you can stay at home with me and go to the community college right up the street. You decide." Everyone left for college. He's like, "I'm getting out, and I'm going to train. And I'm going to get a team." And he literally had a Rolodex of contacts and was on the phone trying to secure a sponsor to go out for a team. He did that himself. And I don't know how many seventeen-year-olds have that ability to do that. He knew what he wanted to do.

ROB: Lance said that there were gallons of sweat over all of the trophies and dollars that he ever earned. I know that he did his first Iron Kids Triathlon when he was about my age—and won it. Did you know at that time what he was going to do with his life?

LINDA KELLY ARMSTRONG: Actually, he came in second place. It was really pretty funny because he was the kid that everybody thought would win. At the time, I think the award was a thousand dollars for second place. And you couldn't take funds if you were going to try and get any kind of college scholarship. That was the biggest quandary he had, "Oh, my goodness. What are we going to do? Take the money and we won't get any scholarship?" So it was hard to envision beyond that.

ROB: By the time Lance was sixteen he was making about twenty thousand dollars racing his bike. Did he contribute to the household expenses?

LINDA KELLY ARMSTRONG: Lance did. Like most young men that are that age, he had a part-time job. He'd work part-time and go to school. In Lance's case that was his part-time job. With that money he would buy designer clothes, or do the things that all the young people were doing with their money at the time. So that was his job. He didn't contribute toward the household expenses as far as maintaining that, but what he did do was buy his school clothes. Just like you would do.

ROB: Was it hard to have him making so much money by just riding a bike when you were working so hard and probably not making a whole lot more?

LINDA KELLY ARMSTRONG: That's a good question. I have to say, when Lance found the team sponsor, and he was seventeen years old, he signed a contract with that team, making more money than I did at the time. And I thought, "That is awesome." Because Lance, when he was young, sixteen, seventeen years old, would take my mother during the week after school to a movie, or to dinner. She had a small Ford Escort. What they did—Lance enjoyed driving around, looking at beautiful homes. He would drive to these beautiful neighborhoods and say to my mother, "Meemaw, I'm going to have a home like that someday." And he was only sixteen years old. He had visions. He had dreams. It makes me proud that he could contribute. You want your kids to do better, and he did. I thought that was pretty cool.

ROB: In what unexpected ways has Lance changed since his cancer?

LINDA KELLY ARMSTRONG: Lance has humbled himself and evolved. It was an evolution of his personal side. We saw, before Lance was sick, a different side of him. It was real hard to get into that. Now you see a very personal, loving, caring connection. And it's humbling.

ROB: Do you know what he wants to be doing ten years from now?

LINDA KELLY ARMSTRONG: I suspect that when his decisions are made to do something different than cycling, that again what he will do is channel those positive energies that he uses on the bike into something. That may be commentating; it could be music. He's got a great network of individuals that he's met. I suspect that he's going to be around more for his family. That's one of the trade-offs he has. It's a sacrifice that he makes.

ROB: Did Lance have any pets when he was my age?

LINDA KELLY ARMSTRONG: He did. We always had a cat. He loves cats. So when he got sick, of course, he got a cat. His name is Chemo.

ROB: What did he do to relax when he was about my age?

LINDA KELLY ARMSTRONG: Lance is like me in a lot of ways. It's hard for us to relax. We never watch TV. I would say he listened to music. He loved music. He loved music.

ROB: Can you think of anything more to tell me about Lance's views when he was my age?

LINDA KELLY ARMSTRONG: I think that it was some of the best times of my life. We were like best friends. And he was so much different, in a lot of ways, than the other people his age. He was an only child. He had a knack for people and great conversations. It's very difficult for young men your age to be able to carry on a conversation with adults, or to acknowledge them first, and show them manners and courtesy. A lot of young men don't have it. That's one of my biggest memories, that he had that courtesy and that love, and could interact with every age, including babies.

ROB: Thank you so much for your time and generosity, for doing this interview.

LINDA KELLY ARMSTRONG: You're welcome.

ROB: Mr. Armstrong, may we ask you a couple of questions? How do you want to be remembered?

LANCE ARMSTRONG: Quite honestly, I don't care about having a long-term legacy. I don't mean that in a bad way. It's just that I think it would be incredibly arrogant to walk through my day thinking about it. That's not why I get up every morning.

ROB: What keeps you motivated, then?

LANCE ARMSTRONG: To train hard and win another bike race. If in fifty years they name a street after me, or build me a statue, that's fine. But quite honestly, I live for these days now. I want my kids to grow up and be normal. I want them to think their father worked hard for what he got, not that it was the result of some kind of magic.

ROB: Do you ever get tired of adhering so rigidly to your training schedules of six to eight hours of biking every day, even when your body is tired and sore?

LANCE ARMSTRONG: It depends whether you want to win. I do. The Tour is a two-thousand-mile race, and people sometimes win by one minute, or less. One minute in nearly a month of suffering isn't that much. So the people who win are the ones willing to suffer the most.

ROB: What goals do you still have for yourself?

LANCE ARMSTRONG: I'm not making plans for postcycling—not yet. That's a bit of a waste of time, I think. Right now I'm hired to do something that I want to do and I believe in, and I don't want any distractions. But, believe me, my life will change drastically. I'll go from living the majority of the year overseas to spending most of my time in Texas with my kids.

ROB: I know that you never knew your father and have referred to him as "the DNA donor." In your book you said, "The main thing you need to know about my childhood is that I never had a real father, but I never sat around wishing for one either. . . . I've never had a single conversation with my mother about him." Do you think you are a good father?

LANCE ARMSTRONG: I'd like to prove I can make a real difference with my cancer foundation. And I'd like to prove I'm a good father. Luke's old enough to understand what's happening. He totally knows. Even the girls. When I put on my bike clothes, they know Daddy's going to work. They know that my bike is my office. It's my job. I love it. And I wouldn't ride if I didn't. But it's incredibly hard work, full of sacrifices. And you have to be able to go out there every single day.

ROB: Do you see Luke on a racing bike someday?

LANCE ARMSTRONG: Whatever he wants to do, I would be totally supportive. If he wants to play the guitar or be a teacher or a lawyer—whatever. He's smart, so maybe he'll do something with his brain. It would be hard for him to race a bike, because of me. I see that now with Eddy Merckx's son. It's tough to grow up doing a sport that your dad did well.

11

Steve Wozniak

S teve Wozniak designed and built and helped to market an entire personal computer (PC), one of the first ever constructed. It was the Apple I. He also designed the Apple II and wrote the software programs to make it run. He is a pioneer in the computer industry who invented many of the parts of computers that we take for granted today. He helped to make *computer* a household word.

Wozniak was born August 11, 1950, in Sunnyvale, California. From the beginning he was fascinated with anything to do with electronics or mathematics. He would sometimes become so immersed in a mathematical problem that his mother would have to physically shake him to bring him back to reality. Because of this passion, he decided as a child that he would become either an engineer or a fifth-grade teacher.

In the mid-1970s Wozniak was an engineering major at the University of California at Berkeley. He decided to drop out and work for Hewlett-Packard, where exciting advances were being made in electronics. At that time computers were in their infancy. They were huge machines that filled whole rooms, generated tremendous heat, and had to be kept in climate-controlled buildings. I have a neighbor who worked with those early computers. He says that they would work wearing only their swim trunks, because the huge computers made the room so hot. Only large universities or corporations could afford to own them.

But there were a lot of people in the San Francisco Bay Area that were interested in computers. Many of them, like Wozniak, formed computer clubs. The Homebrew Computing Club met each week in Palo Alto, and Wozniak became one of its leading members. The atmosphere in the club was casual and mutually supportive. Members shared with each other the advances they were making. Wozniak started working on what would be the Apple I during this time, and he shared the schematics for it with the other club members. They were all content with the joy of discovering new ways to use the amazing technology, and they didn't expect to become rich from the things they were working on. Wozniak, like most of the others, designed his computer simply because he had a passion to see how well he could do it.

In 1975, a man named Steve Jobs began attending the Homebrew Computer Club meetings. He was also interested in computers, but he didn't have the expertise or genius that Wozniak had. Jobs was more interested in marketing, and he saw real potential in these little personal computers. He persuaded Wozniak to work with him toward selling the computers they could make from Wozniak's designs. Together the two men, who were both under twenty-five years old, finished the design for what would be the Apple I in Jobs's bedroom, and they built the prototype in Jobs's family's garage.

As a computer designer, Wozniak believed strongly that simpler and cheaper were better. He bought a twenty-dollar microprocessor for the brain of the computer and searched the surplus market for the cheapest chips he could find to build the computer terminal. His idea of "elegance of design" was to eliminate every wire, connection, and chip possible. He wasn't satisfied with the first design he made. He reworked it again and again in his mind, rearranging the circuitry, until he found a simpler way to get the same result.

In the end his Apple I design, the one he shared for free with other club members, fit onto a single sheet of paper. Although other people were working on the same dream, Wozniak's was among the very first personal computers. Its successor was the Apple II, which made the Apple brand—and personal computers—a household name. Jobs and Wozniak built and sold six hundred Apple I computers for $666 each, mainly to computer hobbyists. About this time Wozniak became known among the club members as "the Wizard of Woz," or "the Woz," to distinguish him from Jobs, because they both were named Steve.

The Apple II offered sound and color and used a television set as its monitor. It did more and was easier to use than anything else on the market, and it cost only $250 to make. It was the bestselling computer for five straight years and earned 139 million dollars! The Apple Computer Company had a growth rate of 700 percent.

Unfortunately, the next two models, the Apple II Plus and the Apple III, didn't enjoy the same amount of popularity as the Apple II had. Then the Apple III had to be recalled in 1981 because of flaws in the design. During this same time the IBM Company gained a large share of the market with its new PC.

As if he didn't have enough problems in 1981, Wozniak's private plane crashed and he suffered a concussion. One of the results of his injury was that Wozniak couldn't make any new memories. He couldn't remember that he had been in an accident. He didn't remember playing games in the hospital on his computer, or who had visited him earlier in the day.

When Wozniak finally recovered from the accident, he decided that the time had come to move away from Apple. For him the thrill had always been in engineering, not in merchandising. So he did many things that he had put off for years. He had decided that he wanted to finally graduate and get his electrical engineering and computer science degrees, so he returned to college at UC Berkeley under the name Rocky Clark (it was a combination of his fiancée's last name and his dog's name). He got married. He also started a company to sponsor music festivals.

After he graduated from college Wozniak decided that he was ready to return to work at Apple, but he wanted to come back in the design department as a regular engineer. So that's what he did. He worked on developing two new computers: the Apple IIe and the Lisa. The Lisa was another groundbreaking computer. It had many brand-new features on it that have since become standard, including a thirty-two-bit processor, a mouse that permitted the user to do graphics production without having to use complicated keyboard entries, and a very sharp video display. It was unfortunate that all the new innovations drove the retail price of the Lisa up to ten thousand dollars each, so it was just too expensive to succeed. But Apple produced a scaled-down model that was called the Macintosh and has done extremely well.

Eventually Wozniak decided to leave Apple. He had enjoyed the engineering challenge much more than the corporate challenges. He left with a personal fortune of about forty-five million dollars, much of which he has given away. He was awarded the National Medal of Technology by President Ronald Reagan in 1985 for his achievements at Apple Computer. It is the highest honor given to America's leaders in technology. In 2000 Wozniak was awarded the Heinz Award for Technology, the Economy and Employment, which is a prestigious award. That same year he was also inducted into the Inventors Hall of Fame.

Since he left Apple, Wozniak has spent much of his time volunteering in schools. He regularly teaches fifth graders and their teachers in his hometown of Los Gatos, California. He had his own computer lab built at his home so that the students can come to him to be taught, but he also has built whole computer labs at schools. He gives computers and Internet accounts to students. He then teaches classes on basic computer usage, lessons on how to program, and classes on network topics. Wozniak has given hundreds of laptop computers to local students. He is currently writing a book about his life. He is also the founder, chairman, and CEO of Wheels of Zeus (wOz), which is involved in creating new electronic products.

He is a generous philanthropist and is hugely respected. He founded the Electronic Frontier Foundation and was a founding sponsor of the Children's Discovery Museum of San Jose, the Silicon Valley Ballet, and the Tech Museum.

Wozniak believes in encouraging freethinking and creativity in children. He speaks to them about avoiding drugs, which rob them of being the master of their own fate, and about fighting the "forces of conformity." Steve Wozniak is such a hero to me. I love how he turned his passion with electronics and engineering into a business that has improved the lives of millions of people. I admire his generosity, in both freely sharing his innovations with the Homebrew Computer Club and giving away most of the fortune that he made. I admire his honesty in recognizing that he enjoys teaching more than he enjoys being head of a huge corporation. I don't think many people would be willing to give up what he walked away from at Apple. And I appreciate how approachable he is. He is always open to meeting people and helping them.

How Rob Got the Interview

Wozniak was one of just three of the heroes who responded personally to the first letter I sent. I actually sent it in an e-mail, because I found an address on his website. At the same time, I sent the letter addressed to Wozniak to about twenty-five other people that I had identified as having some connection to him, asking each one to please send the letter on to Wozniak. That had become my standard procedure. And I felt unusually lucky if the first batch of letters produced any result. Usually those first twenty-five letters would be just the first step in trying to make contact with the hero. But in this case I heard from Wozniak about two days later. His e-mail said, "Well, I think we ought to do it," and told me to arrange a time with his secretary.

So my brother-in-law and I flew to San Jose, California. The next day we set out for our lunch appointment with Wozniak. Even though our hotel was only three miles away, it took us forty-five minutes to find his office. We actually passed it twice. There were trees in front of the sign. His office was remarkably small and not fancy. The secretary out front was kind but protective, like a doorkeeper.

His office seemed full of neat technological stuff, including two Segway personal transportation devices propped against the wall, which he allowed us to try. Then the three of us walked down the street to a little soup and sandwich shop.

I was impressed by how very kind and open Wozniak seemed. After we were finished with the interview we discussed video games. My brother-in-law gave a very strongly worded attack on the game Pong, not realizing that Wozniak had created that game! I was pretty embarrassed, but Wozniak just let it slide.

◆

Interview

Coffee shop, Los Gatos, California, March 10, 2003

ROB: So, first off, I'd like to thank you for meeting with us today. You are the first person that we asked to interview that actually responded to me personally, not through a secretary.

STEVE WOZNIAK: Normally, for people your age, I would be willing to fly out and see *you* guys.

ROB: Really?

STEVE WOZNIAK: Yeah. Younger people deserve a little special attention now and then, that they wouldn't think they'd get. So, it's neat to see you here.

ROB: I appreciate that. When you left Apple you had amassed somewhere between 45 and 200 million dollars—depending on which news article you read. Different articles have different figures.

STEVE WOZNIAK: I did not technically leave Apple. I stayed on the payroll as an employee at all times. I was never disloyal. There were misquotes in newspapers that made it sound like I had gripes and was leaving. That was never the case.

One of the times I had a plane crash and wanted to go back to college. I didn't leave Apple. Another time I wanted to start another small company—an experience that I like so much—to make remote controls. I did not leave Apple.

ROB: You've had the same phone number for about twenty years. You have just one e-mail address which your friends use, and your home address and everything is still available on your website. Why are you so accessible to people you don't know?

STEVE WOZNIAK: It was in my background that one of my values was always to be accessible and open. You read about people who hide out and become so important that they can't be reached. But there is still a balance, because sometimes when I'm in the news I get a ton of e-mail, just way too much for any human being to answer. And other times I get very difficult e-mail. They expect me to know things I don't know, and to do the research that they could do, and to take the time. It's so difficult when they expect that I have a bunch of answers when I don't really have the time for it. Sometimes I can't get to all my e-mails, but I try to.

ROB: OK. You've given away over seven million dollars.

STEVE WOZNIAK: Oh, no, no, no. Dozens of millions. To arts groups in San Jose, California, to museums, to individuals (like computers to schools). I've given millions to a bunch of USSR things, back before the coup. I was sponsoring a lot of person-to-person diplomacy—feeling that was the best way to overcome the cold war.

Some people that continued in business became billionaires eventually. But my ideals led me to give the bulk of my wealth away, and not that much remains.

ROB: What has led to your being so generous to so many people?

STEVE WOZNIAK: I just grew up with that whole value, and I'm not sure where it comes from. I can't go back. A lot of my values I can trace back to conversations with my father. And how they got into me? Some people just grow up wanting to be helpful—I just didn't want to gather riches and grow new riches from them. I didn't want to start a company. I turned it down for that reason. I felt a little unethical about it.

My goal in life was to be a good designer. There are a lot of good people with good ideas. And I was lucky.

ROB: As you know, my book is about my heroes.

STEVE WOZNIAK: I wonder why, when I just did kind of normal things—some good engineering and just what I wanted to do in life—why everywhere I go, some people think that I'm some kind of hero or a special person. People want to say it's one special person in the world that does the good thing. But it's really the body of people and their mass thinking that caused computers to happen. But you always want to pinpoint a few individuals and say this is why. That is dodging the fact that all people, really, were going that way. There was a long development of technology that was leading to what we have today.

ROB: I know you liked the Tom Swift books, but what were your favorite books [when you were] about ages eleven to fourteen?

STEVE WOZNIAK: I remember Tom Swift. I do not remember a lot of other books I read around that time. Maybe around age fourteen—freshman in high school—I do remember reading *Walden Pond*, and that affected me quite a bit to this day. A lot of my personality comes from what I read in that book. I don't remember too many others that well. Not too long after that time, of course, I read *Lord of the Rings*. That was my favorite book my whole life.

ROB: What makes you angry? I've read a lot about you, and I just keep finding like three different books will say three completely different things about you.

STEVE WOZNIAK: Basically, books on Apple—I never read them. They are almost always wrong. They are off. It's just worthless to really believe. It's history. When you're reading it you believe it, but it's just too worthless.

As far as what gets me mad—actually nothing. People will tell you that I just don't ever get upset at things. That's not quite true—I'll explain. Everyone comes up with his or her own keys to happiness in life, which is the important thing. It's not how much money you have; it's not what prestigious things you've done. It's how happy you've been in your life—how many times you've smiled and laughed. To me, a lot of it was just that not getting into arguments. So I'm nonpolitical—I don't get psyched on issues.

It does bother me, though, that I put so much into the early Apple dreams—the Macintosh Lisa computer—that the computer software should work with human beings on a human level. And when I see the way the software is so extraordinarily nonintuitive and complicated, that bothers me.

Also when I see injustices to other people—usually in a civil liberties sense. My dad taught me that we have a great country that's a democracy. We have freedom to say what you feel. You can even criticize the president of the United States if you want to. It's your right. You can't do that in other countries. To see that trashed—that sort of thing, over and over—I'll see it happen now and then. I feel very sorry and bad about it. I try to help when I can.

ROB: I've read a lot of things about practical jokes that you've pulled, and things like that. What would you say that your favorite, or biggest, practical joke was?

STEVE WOZNIAK: I have so many that are so big. I have hundreds that nobody knows about to this day. There are a lot of good ones—tons of them that are basketball things, tons with two-dollar bills. Two-dollar bills, because I figure that unusual things are interesting. So I get two-dollar bills on sheets, gummed into a check pad, perforated between the bills like green stamps. They look just weird enough that they got me a long talk with the Secret Service. But I gave them a fake ID that said "Laser Safety Officer," and I had an eye patch in the picture. That was a funny one. Going back to high school—probably the greatest, that never came off, was with Steve Jobs. We were trying to turn the sprinklers on the audience at graduation on the football field. And we even epoxied the thing shut so that even the janitors wouldn't be able to turn it off. We came close. We came close to pulling that off.

ROB: When you were in high school, you played sports. You swam, played baseball, and all that. From what I've read it seemed that your life was pretty balanced.

STEVE WOZNIAK: And I lettered in pole-vaulting. I love the pole vault. What a fun sport. You can never imagine. Running down and zooming up in the air, and flopping down. The only other thing that fun would be springboard diving.

I was real lucky. I was real good at Little League, and swimming. I admire sports, and I have a couple of real good athlete children. My daughter is a national diver. She had her choice of colleges. And I have a son who's a league champion right here at Los Gatos High in wrestling.

ROB: You have mentioned that Bob Dylan was one of your heroes when you were about my age, because of what he was saying.

STEVE WOZNIAK: Largely the words of his songs. And a lot of his songs were spoken songs—talking through the songs. His early folk stuff was so incredibly good. You know what? When I listen to it now, I realize that that's probably the closest thing to what musicians are trying to do with rap music today.

He was on some very important themes. He would talk about people who had suffered injustices and got unfair prison penalties for just a car going out of control and plowing into people or something. He took sides of other people.

ROB: Have you ever met him?

STEVE WOZNIAK: I never met him. I've had the opportunity to, but some people are too much of a hero. You're almost afraid to approach them. And I didn't have the nerve to really go up and approach him and talk to him. But I collect books of his lyrics. And still admire certain older phrases of his. And I'm impressed with what he can do to this day.

ROB: And Fred Rogers, who just died.

STEVE WOZNIAK: Fred Rogers was sort of a hero of mine. They had a show once called "Fred Rogers' Heroes." This was on heroes. And he told me that if they ever did that show again, I would be on it. Because when he came to San Jose I got to meet him and speak to him, and I explained to him how I was the one who had funded the Children's Discovery Museum. I told him I'd done all my schooling, and told him what my beliefs were about education and young children. And he was actually kind of impressed with that.

And, of course, everyone is impressed with who he is. He was an excellent speaker. It was sad to see him pass away. He was a great man. He left a lot of greatness.

ROB: What was it like to have Dana Carvey write a song about you?

STEVE WOZNIAK: I barely met Dana Carvey. There was actually an Apple show where he did a whole comedy skit about "the Woz." And for some reason I was sick and didn't go that night. I don't remember the song you're talking about. But even halfway musicians have written a few songs. Some have even been on records. One's even been written by one of my children. No big deals or anything, but nice songs.

ROB: Who are your heroes today?

STEVE WOZNIAK: Jimmy Carter has always been my top hero. He's an ethical, moral, untainted key person that other people would know.

It's a difficult question because I might have them and just not be able to pin it down right here and now. As far as business heroes, I would say, certainly, Steve Jobs, because he holds out to do the best job possible, in this modern day of companies controlling computers, to create different, special stuff where everybody else is just kind of status quo, least common denominator, cheap commodity–type product. And I think he's a hero in that sense. I like what's coming out of Apple.

John Kerry is certainly my biggest hero, for standing up to some difficult times.

ROB: You said that you hope people will remember you as a great engineer and a great person, that you cared too much about people to be involved in politics or business. Is that how you'd like to be remembered?

STEVE WOZNIAK: Yes. It hasn't changed my whole life, really. I'm kind of one of those lucky people who sort of figured out what I wanted in life by about sixth grade. And amazingly, all those things, the top level of them all, happened to me, just like that. I never really had to worry about where am I going, what am I going to do, because I had so much electronics knowledge that I always had a job. And electronics and computers are so important to me. And teaching. Especially being good with other people. I've done all these things. So I couldn't have a better life. I don't have much money left, but the life's the important part.

ROB: How do you feel about the MP3 copyrights and everything?

STEVE WOZNIAK: If I buy software, I buy five copies for five computers. I will never buy one and try to share it around.

I'm extremely ethical, and I teach this to all my kids in class. If you want something, you pay for it. Music, though, is very difficult, because the whole thing about copyright boils down to agreements between parties—essentially, contracts. You buy something, you have a license, you have to follow these terms. You made an agreement to follow these terms. It's like your contract with society. You will obey the law. The copyright is so strict you can't do anything with it. You can't agree to something that is so unreasonable it makes no sense. I can have a piece of music, and I can't even back it up. I have a piece of music and I can't make a copy for myself. There are so many justifications for being able to copy songs freely on computers, the easy way. When I was young I would buy a record, and I would tape it on a reel-to-reel tape recorder, because I was one of the few people in the world that owned one. And then I would, strictly for money, sell the album. And I'd still have the tape, not that I listened to it much. But today that would be illegal. I don't think it was then. I think there was a principle. I've talked to so many lawyers and other people, and nobody has one answer.

It's just like what seems logical to a child is probably what the law should be. What's intuitive is what the law should be. Being able to copy something good that you have, and share it with a friend, I don't really think it's as economically disastrous as it's made out to be.

But I do dislike the fact that college kids go around copying every single thing they can find, whether they want it or not. We have these guys with computers today. They copy games software. Now they copy all this music and get a big collection. Let's say they copy anything they can, and they're not going to have to buy anything. They've got all the music they need. There's an ethical problem with that, because they now feel that anything they can get away with, and that you know you can't get caught for, is OK. It's OK to steal anything if you can't get caught and nobody will ever know. And it's just a wrong message to give, especially to youth.

I just believe in being more honest. And that's the problem that's the natural outcome of this whole thing. If we just got rid of the MP3 copyright laws, nobody would be guilty of anything. And there's a lot of good reason to think the music industry would be as healthy as it is.

There are two sides of the music industry. You have to admit, it has the right to decide what they're going to do with their product, what terms they're going to put on it, if they believe they'll be better off with Napster, or worse off. They have the right to decide, and we don't.

There's a little bit of unfairness, legally. First of all, if you bought a record thirty years ago when the laws were different, you should have different rights over that. You should have the right to do what the law was when you bought it. So it's not fair to come and take that right away at a later date when you paid your money at an earlier date. You kept your agreement—they should keep theirs. That's a legal principle of the grandfather clause also. The music industry has evolved to a point where there's a whole bunch of narrow types

of channels, narrow types of music each selling their own thing. So
the record companies don't have to look for good music—establish
an artist and crank out their stuff, and that's all that you let get
played. All the radio stations are paid money to play only these few
choices from the record companies. And I guarantee, those are the
ones that will sell. Music is supposed to be like an invention—
taking us to a new place in life and in the world. That doesn't happen. And we got here through a long process of developing an industry with a few very strong record company players, and a lot of
control and ownership of places like Clear Channel, and the radio
stations, and the music business. And they're all in this one little neat
thing where they can turn a crank and keep cranking out money, and
not an innovation survives.

When you listen to a college station, which I do all the time, you
hear this unbelievable, incredible stuff from the United States and
around the world. It's so good. When I was a kid, you heard all that
good stuff. One channel played every type of music. As long as it
was good, you heard it.

It's really in sad shape where it's just mediocrity that's manufac-
tured. A lot of artists have spoken out. One of the real notable ones
was Don Henley, who had a very good article about this.

This is one of the things that bothers me—the way the music
industry is structured now. OK, let's say that another company starts
up and says, "We'll be the company that lets people copy our stuff
on Napster." The company will probably fail because of the system
that's evolved already; they don't have control over what you hear
on the radio. They don't have control over what you'll encounter at
concert venues. Over what you'll see in record stores. Because the
other companies are already in control of that.

In other words, the competition and the free choice of people that
would have taken place maybe twenty or thirty years ago, right now
it's not free, fair competition between a free music company and one
that has control and won't let you copy freely, because the industry
has evolved in the way it did. And we should have things equivalent
to hiring quotas and that kind of a thing—incentives that kind of
equalize the trade-offs, so people can at least have those choices and

see which they prefer. Right now all they have is a random, free, little tiny group on the Internet somewhere. But there's no good, solid way to get the best of the best from reliable trusted sources. And they can't compete today because they can't get into the channels and money keeps them out.

ROB: OK. I know that this is kind of jumping from topic to topic, but do you believe in God?

STEVE WOZNIAK: What?

ROB: God.

STEVE WOZNIAK: God?

ROB: Yeah.

STEVE WOZNIAK: I have my own definition. I think that the word *God* and the word *nature* are interchangeable in almost any discussion between different people. I just believe that God is a set of principles in your own brain. For me, it's in my brain. My brain is smart enough to figure out that good principles have been good to people. And I call that my God. It's something I look to as guiding principles. I don't believe in God the way most people would, which is in an organized religion sense. Because I don't feel like someone else should tell me, "Oh, you have to believe this in this religion." And another religion says, "We believe this way." Think for yourself. I'm not a puppet who follows somebody else telling me what to think. Thoreau was a big influence in that direction—going back to ninth grade.

ROB: That is all of my questions. I really appreciate you meeting with us.

12

Dolores Huerta

Dolores Fernandez Huerta cofounded the United Farm Workers of America (UFW) with Cesar Chavez and has worked tirelessly for more than fifty years to help migrant farmworkers gain basic rights and justice.

She was born in 1930 in Dawson, New Mexico. Her mother and her maternal grandparents had also been born in New Mexico. Her father's parents emigrated from Mexico before her father was born.

When Huerta was very young her parents divorced and she moved with her mom and two brothers to Stockton, California, where she lived in a neighborhood full of people of all races. She enjoyed knowing people of Filipino, Chinese, Japanese, Jewish, and Mexican heritage. Her father, who had remained in New Mexico, became active in labor unions, eventually graduated from college, and became a representative in the New Mexico state legislature. Her mother ran a hotel and restaurant in Stockton.

After Huerta graduated from the University of the Pacific's Delta College, she began teaching school. She was frustrated that she couldn't do more to help the children who came to her class barefoot and hungry. Eventually she left teaching and began to work for a Mexican-American self-help association called the Community Service Organization, which had been organized by Fred Ross in Los Angeles. Huerta worked as a lobbyist for the organization in California's capital city of Sacramento. She registered people to vote, and she organized citizenship classes for immigrants.

As Huerta became acquainted with immigrant farmworkers, she was touched by the harsh conditions in which they lived and worked. They worked in the hot sun picking grapes, tomatoes, and other crops. Often they slept in their cars or in run-down shacks. They were paid low wages—often only twenty or fifty cents for each basket of produce they picked. Some owners paid even less, and some owners subtracted from their pay for any water the worker had drunk during the shift! Many of the farmworkers were Mexican or Filipino, and most of them spoke little English. Some of the farm owners took advantage of that and paid the workers even less than had been promised to them.

Huerta eventually founded the Agricultural Workers Association, a community interest group in Northern California. While there she met Cesar Chavez, who was also concerned about the plight of farmworkers.

Cesar Chavez and Dolores Huerta together finally started the National Farm Workers Association in Delano, California, in 1962. In 1967 it known as the United Farm Workers. Today the group has seventy thousand members.

In 1935 the National Labor Relations Act had become law in the United States. It gave most workers the right to organize in unions. Only farmworkers, government workers, and railroad and airline workers were not guaranteed that right. Dolores Huerta was determined to change that.

Three years after the National Farm Workers Association was started, they began the famous Delano Grape Strike. It lasted for five years, and five thousand grape workers walked off their jobs. Huerta, along with Chavez and other union officials, led the workers on the picket lines. Huerta was a young mother, and she often had some of her little children with her. She became the union's first contract negotiator, the person who would meet with the corporate lawyers and farm owners to try and work out acceptable contracts. Huerta also spent a year during the strike living in New York City while directing the grape boycott on the East Coast, which is the primary distribution point for grapes.

Huerta was able to help bring about a successful grape boycott throughout the country. She united many different groups including feminists, religious groups, peace groups, community workers, and student protesters. They all worked together in fighting for the rights of migrant farmworkers.

Huerta worked out the first United Farm Workers of California contract in 1966 with the Schenley Wine Company. It was an amazing accomplishment. It was the first time in American history that farmworkers were able to negotiate a collective bargaining agreement with an agricultural corporation. Collective bargaining means that one person, in this case Dolores Huerta, talks on behalf of all the workers and has the authority to make an agreement with management. The ability to do collective bargaining is almost sure to guarantee to workers a more advantageous deal. After the agreements were reached, Huerta was the one who administered them. She conducted more than a hundred grievance procedures for the workers.

Slowly the working situation for migrant farmworkers began to change. In 1975 California passed the Agricultural Labor Relations Act. It was the first bill of rights for farmworkers that had ever been enacted in America. It gave farmworkers the right to form a union that could negotiate with farm owners for better working conditions and pay.

In the years since then Huerta has continued her uncompromising fight for justice for farmworkers and for women. She has testified before state and federal committees about a number of issues. She spoke against the use of toxic pesticides on crops and how DDT and other pesticides are very harmful to the farmworkers who have to work with the crops after the pesticide has been applied. She has also testified about other health concerns of farmworkers.

Although she has always been immersed in her union activities, Huerta has also managed to raise eleven children. She was twenty years old when her first child was born and was forty-six when her last one was born. She now also has fourteen grandchildren and four great-grandchildren.

Huerta didn't want to choose between going to work or being with her children, so she took them to work with her. When they were old enough, she would put them to work as well. When the union was first started, Huerta had been divorced twice and had seven young children. They would all pack into the car with her when she drove around visiting migrant farm labor camps. And they moved across the country with her when she led grape boycotts in New York City, Los Angeles, and Chicago.

In 1988 Huerta was one of hundreds of people participating in a peaceful demonstration in San Francisco. They were protesting the politics of George H. W. Bush, who was running for president. Police officers with batons closed in on the protest, and Huerta was severely injured. She had a ruptured spleen and two broken ribs. She underwent emergency surgery to save her life.

Luckily someone had caught on videotape the attack on Huerta. When the tape was broadcast, the country was outraged. The San Francisco Police Department was forced to change its policies about crowd control and had to pay damages to Huerta.

Cesar Chavez and Dolores Huerta worked together for more than thirty years. In those years they were able to create the first pension plan, credit union, and medical plan for farmworkers. The U.S. Immigration Act of 1985 was one result of their work; it granted amnesty for farmworkers who had worked, lived, and paid taxes in the United States for many years but were unable to become citizens because they were in the country illegally.

Another project they worked on together was the National Farm Workers Service Center. It provided community-based affordable housing.

Dolores Huerta is proud that she and Chavez were able to demonstrate to the world that social change can happen without violence. She has received many awards and honors. She was named in the *Ladies Home Journal* as one of the one hundred most important women of the twentieth century. In 1999 she received the Eleanor Roosevelt Human Rights Award from President Bill Clinton. Huerta has also been given the Ellis Island Medal of Freedom Award.

In recent years Huerta has continued to work for inclusion in American society of farmworkers and of women. She points out that there is still a lot to do. For example, in California alone there are only nineteen inspectors for thirty-six thousand agricultural work sites. One-third of vineyard employers don't pay their employees the minimum wage. Only a quarter of farmworkers make more than ten thousand dollars each year.

I love Dolores Huerta's enthusiasm and passion. You might think that over fifty years the fight would kind of go out of her. But she is still walking in protest marches and helping people who had no voice until she came along to help them help themselves. My aunt Jan has idolized Huerta for a long time, and she suggested that I study about her.

I was amazed at what she, with the help of other key people, has accomplished. Thousands of people live easier and safer lives now because of her sacrifices. I love it that she didn't decide between the union and her family but managed to raise her children while fulfilling the obligations she'd made for herself in organized labor.

How Rob Got the Interview

From the very first time that Will sat down to name his heroes, Cesar Chavez was on his list. Unfortunately, Chavez died in 1993. It was years later that my aunt, who is active in union politics, suggested Dolores Huerta. I'm sorry to say that I had never even heard of her.

But as I read about her I was just amazed at her dedication and at all the years that she has devoted to the farmworkers. I knew that I really wanted to meet and interview her.

As usual, I began writing letters. Among the ones I sent was one that my aunt forwarded through union channels. My aunt's roommate forwarded another one through people she knew. I wrote to the lawyer of the UFW and to Huerta at a UFW address and other possible addresses. I don't know which letter got through to her, but her daughter, Camilla Chavez, called to set up a meeting.

Huerta travels so much that it was very hard to find a time when I could catch her. Finally we agreed on the day before Easter. That was perfect for me, since I would be on spring break from school. We would meet in Bakersfield, California, which is where Huerta lives.

When I told my mom the plans, she decided that we would drive to Bakersfield from Utah—that way we could also take my little brother to Disneyland. Mom has driven to southern California lots of times, and the interstate goes right through Bakersfield.

So we went to California. The idea appealed to my uncle and his family, so they came, too. We invited my niece along. Then my grandparents decided that they didn't want to miss any fun. In all, fourteen of us made the trip in three separate cars. We were going to meet with Huerta on our way home.

As we drove south, Mom noticed that we were driving through *Baker*, California, not *Bakersfield*! This was a real surprise. And then, when we double-checked with Chavez, she asked to postpone the interview until the day after Easter. So my older brother flew home so he wouldn't miss any school, and we drove two hundred miles farther than we had thought we would need to and got home two days later than planned.

But, as you will see, the interview was really worth it. We met in the lobby of the hotel in Bakersfield where my family stayed. Chavez accompanied her mother. Huerta was a tiny, intense, wrinkled, feisty person. She laughed a lot as we talked. I could tell that she just loved the things she was doing. Maybe that is part of why she has been so successful.

◆

Interview

BAKERSFIELD, CALIFORNIA, APRIL 21, 2003

ROB: Thank you so much for meeting with me. Thank you for your time. As you know, my book is about heroes and what their lives were like when they were around my age—eleven to fourteen. I know that you helped your mom in her hotel, and that you were a very good student. What were some of your favorite books during that period?

DOLORES HUERTA: Oh gosh. I read every book in the library [laughs]. Know what I mean? I read so many books. I read detective stories a lot, maybe when I was a little bit younger—maybe about twelve. Nancy Drew stories. I think I was about twelve when I read Nancy Drew. Adventure stories a lot.

I used to like Rudyard Kipling—you know, *The Jungle Book*. I read a lot of Pearl Buck. My mother used to work, so when I got done with school I'd go straight to the library and stay there until it closed. By the time the library closed my mother was home. We lived only four or five blocks from the public library. I lived at the library, and I almost read every single book in the library [laughs], you know?

I liked the myths a lot—the myths of the Greek gods. I liked that. I liked folk stories a lot. *Little Women* by Louisa May Alcott was one of my favorite books. Another one that I read about ten times was *Ramona* by Helen Hunt Jackson. All of the Huckleberry Finn and Tom Sawyer books were favorites.

ROB: You seem to have such an amazing amount of energy. I read that your daughter said you're like a character from "Star Trek"— you don't really need sleep or food.

DOLORES HUERTA: That's actually more before. I was sick a couple of years ago—I had an aneurism and almost died. I was disabled for almost a whole year. So now I do need to eat and sleep. I wish I didn't have to that much, you know. I wish I could go on and on, and not have to worry about eating and sleeping.

ROB: When I read about you doing the 165-mile march in 2002 to demand that California's Governor Davis sign a bill about mediation for farmworkers—it just kind of blew me away. I did a trek with my church, and it was just three days—probably twenty miles a day—but it about wore me out. Many people my age would not want to do an eleven-day 165-mile march, no matter how important the cause. Did you have a lot of energy when you were my age?

DOLORES HUERTA: Yes, I did. But I was actually kind of a quiet person. I did a lot of dancing, took dancing and music lessons. But I didn't think of myself as being super energetic. I think it's more like being able to hang in there, you know what I mean? I know you asked, when you wrote, if I'm attention deficit. I'm not a hyper person. I just have a lot of tenacity, or staying-in kind of power, that kind of thing. Three of my children are very high energy. But I'm not high energy like they are. They can't stay still. They have to be doing something. I'm not like that. I can sit still. I do think I have a lot of staying power. We actually did another march that was 250 miles. And we did have young people that marched with us, that were your age.

ROB: I know that you studied music when you were my age, and that you played violin and took dance lessons. How do you feel about those different things? Were they a bother to you?

DOLORES HUERTA: Oh, no. I think of music and dancing as extremely important. I think that one of the unfortunate things that we have in our country right now is that because of the budget costs, and because we're putting our money in other things like wars, we don't have music lessons and art lessons and dance lessons for children. Because I think that's a very important part of a person's personality. And one of the things that I regret that I was not able to give my children, because of the fact that when I worked for the union we didn't have wages, I wasn't able to provide my children with that type of activity. But I think it's very important. And I think it's a part of education that should be provided free for all students.

ROB: What was your favorite kind of dance that you studied?

DOLORES HUERTA: Well, I did flamenco, and ballet, and tap. And I still love flamenco very much. And I like salsa, you know, and I also took a lot of Mexican folk dancing. So I love all kinds of dancing, because I love to dance. It's kind of a tradition in our family that we're all dancers.

ROB: You said about your school years that it didn't matter whether your grades were good or not. If you were black or brown you got treated differently. I'm a white kid from a state that has a minority population of only about 12 percent.

DOLORES HUERTA: Yes. I remember the Olympics, and the joking that one of the guys from Jamaica was the only black guy there.

ROB: I only know about two other kids my age very well that are of other nationalities or races. How would you suggest that someone like me make more friends from other different backgrounds?

DOLORES HUERTA: Well I think, first of all, that it's important to do. People of color are 75 percent of the world. Anglo-Saxons are only 25 percent. And so they are, right now, a minority in the world. And it's very difficult, I think, for Anglos to understand other people and other cultures when they don't know anybody of any other culture. And they have so many wrong ideas. And racism is harmful.

I'll give you a good example right now, with the war that we've been having. It's really easy for people to connect Osama bin Laden with Saddam Hussein, although they are two different people who are actually enemies of each other. But because they are both Arab, and they are both brown, people think that certainly they must be the same. This whole stereotyping of people of color, especially thinking they are all criminals, or illegal aliens, or drug dealers, or whatever, it's very harmful to our society.

And so, I think one way it can be overcome is that in our school systems, again, we insist on having ethnic studies as part of the education, so people can learn about the contributions of African-Americans and Latino-Americans and Asian-Americans and women to our society.

Maybe exchange programs. We just came from a meeting, just now, where there was a group of young people from Mexico who are studying to be teachers. They are staying at the Days Inn. We just came from meeting those people. I think that if you can't find them in your own state, well maybe you need to go to New Mexico or some state, so that you can start meeting people from other cultures. It's very very important.

You have a lot of farmworkers in Idaho and Utah, by the way, who are Mexican immigrants. I've been there, and spoken at some of their events that they've had there. You have to go out of your way to meet some of those folks.

ROB: OK. At one point when you were in high school, you created a place for kids to hang out after school. You got furniture and games donated, and kids from a wide range of backgrounds came. But the police shut it down. Why did they do that?

DOLORES HUERTA: Because they didn't like to see the Anglo kids hanging around with the black kids and the Mexican kids and the Asian kids.

ROB: Looking back on that experience, do you think the same thing would happen today?

DOLORES HUERTA: Probably. I think it might happen again today. We still have a lot of racism, unfortunately. Probably in Utah it would [laughs].

ROB: Yeah. That's very true. Who were your heroes when you were my age?

DOLORES HUERTA: Of course, one's parents are always one's heroes, right? My mother definitely was mine.

You know, there were hardly any models that one could think about. We'd go to the movies and you always saw that all of the Indians got killed, and they looked like us.

My heroes were all the musicians, the people that were making jazz music and swing music—Duke Ellington and Charlie Parker and

Dizzy Gillespie. Those were definitely my heroes. And Lena Horne. They were mostly people of color. I can remember looking up to them, or wanting to be with them, or paying money to go to the dances to hear them.

One very important person was my Girl Scout leader, Kathryn Kemp. She was my Girl Scout leader from the time I was eight until I was eighteen. She was definitely my hero.

ROB: You've spent basically fifty years with all your energy focused toward basically one goal—the equality of farmworkers' pay and everything. Do you ever wonder if it was worth it?

DOLORES HUERTA: Actually, there are two goals, Robby—equality of farmworkers, and also the equality of women. So I have two goals. And definitely it has been worth it because we've been able to accomplish a lot on both fronts—both in getting farmworkers better wages and better working conditions. We've passed laws, like unemployment insurance in California (not in Utah), workers' comp, the farmworkers' right to organize. So I think it's been very well worth it. Do you know there are families out there that have more food on the table because of it? I just met a woman who told me that her grandfather got a pension from the union—and it will continue every month until he dies. And that was because he was a farmworker under a union contract.

ROB: That's really cool. Do you ever wake up in the morning and think, "I'll just sleep and read a book instead of picketing or whatever"?

DOLORES HUERTA: We don't picket every day. One has to take time out to recoup, and to rest, and to hear music and go dancing, right? Definitely! I like to do that as often as I can. I'm not always able to. Today is my day off, and yesterday was Easter, and we had all our family together for Easter Sunday. It was nice.

ROB: I read that you were one of the people who was actually with Robert Kennedy minutes before he was shot. Can you tell me what that was like?

DOLORES HUERTA: Well, it was horrible, because we had such hopes that we would have a good president who would lead us in the right direction. And we lost him. People kind of went berserk in the hotel. They started throwing furniture, and doing all kinds of wild things. It was really very, very sad. And to this day, I think our country lost a great leader. It was very sad.

ROB: I know that you've been arrested more than twenty-three times and have been physically attacked at least once, and probably more times. Was that day with Robert Kennedy the most afraid that you've been?

DOLORES HUERTA: I don't think I was afraid. I was not afraid. The time I was the most afraid is one time when someone came to my house at three o'clock in the morning and knocked on my door and said, "Helen sent me. She's my wife." And so I opened the door but left it on the latch, because my son is very conservative and put the latch on. When I opened the door this fellow tried to push the door, but because we had the latch on, the door sprung back. And then he proceeded to break our windows throughout the house, and I got really terrified because my son was sleeping on the sofa, right under the window. The window shattered, and all the glass went all over the sofa. He jumped out of the way in time, but I screamed. And then, whoever these terrorists were, were going around my house, and my little dog was barking, and they were kicking the dog, and the dog was crying. I had two of my sons at home with me, and I put one up to the window in the bathroom to see out and just braced myself at the bathroom door in case they tried to come in. My son said that there were two men in a black car. They were trying to get into some of the other windows of the house. The ones that they broke they couldn't enter through because the windows shattered and they couldn't put their hands through. That was the most scared I've ever been.

When Bobby Kennedy died it was just such a trauma. We were all shocked, you know? I wasn't so much afraid as I was numb. I didn't feel any personal fear; I just heard the bullets flying. The magnitude of what was happening was just so bad. So horrible. I was kind of in shock.

ROB: One of the books I read said that everyone in the UFW is a volunteer. No one is paid a salary, like you also said. The union just paid staff's rent, food, and medical expenses. It said that it has always been your philosophy that you can't help farmworkers if you are so much richer than they are. How does that work if one of your daughters wants a prom dress, or one of your kids really wants to take ballet lessons?

DOLORES HUERTA: Well, I kind of answered that one earlier. But the union doesn't work that way anymore. You should be aware of that. They do now pay the organizers. And I am not working for the union anymore. I resigned a few years ago. But that was Cesar's philosophy. He didn't want the organizers to be too much above where the workers were, or above at all where the workers were. And it worked very well for many, many years. The one problem that the union had was that you'd have other unions that would come and hire our organizers because they were so good! And so we were always losing organizers. So now the union is actually paying the organizers—although not as much, probably, as other unions do.

The one thing that's important, and that might fall into some of your other questions, is that the important thing to give your children is values. Not so much material goods. People think that you've got to give your children a lot of toys, a lot of designer clothes. What they need are values in order to have respect for themselves. They need to know how to fight for themselves, how to fight for justice. Involve them in what you're doing so they'll grow up with that as a lifestyle, to give them courage and strength. That's the most important thing. Not material goods.

ROB: I know that after the police in San Francisco attacked you, in 1988, you sued them and settled for about $825,000. You stated that you were going to donate the money to the union, which I know is also what you've done with other awards that you've won, such as the $100,000 Puffin Prize given to you by the Nation Institute. Didn't you keep any of it for yourself?

DOLORES HUERTA: Well, actually, the $100,000 Puffin Prize I'm using to start an organization—the Dolores Huerta Foundation—and we're going to be using that money to train organizers. We're trying to raise more money so that we can do it a second year.

ROB: Books describe Cesar Chavez as being quiet and shy. But, in spite of that, he is the one that most people identify with the United Farm Workers. One magazine even said that the police and the FBI know more about you than the average history student does. How do you feel about that?

DOLORES HUERTA: I think it's just the way history usually is. They call it "his-story," and not "her-story," right? I think that often what happens is that women, especially, they are not included in the history of an organization. Although I think that's changing now, with the women's movement. Like your coming here today, they are focusing more on the contributions women have made to various movements.

It's kind of a natural thing because Cesar was a really great person. He was the leader of the organization. And he did these incredible things. So I think it's good that history has recognized what he's done. And everything that Cesar and I did, it was also thousands of farmworkers that were out there marching, and going to the state capitol with flags, and doing all this work.

You know, a stamp is going to be issued in his name on the twenty-third of April. There's going to be all kinds of celebrations throughout the country. I'm going down to Los Angeles to do the issue of the stamp there on Wednesday. It will probably be in the news—so just watch the news for that.

ROB: Speaking of the FBI, I know that the FBI's surveillance continued on with you and the UFW movement for more than ten years. They even noted that you were the driving force on the picket lines. At the time, were you aware of the FBI surveillance?

DOLORES HUERTA: No. I think we had suspicions, because we always had some people that acted really weird, you know what I mean? But we didn't know for sure. I think that it wasn't until afterward that all this stuff came out. I didn't even know that quote that you had there about myself.

ROB: How did the FBI surveillance affect your family and your kids?

DOLORES HUERTA: I don't think they've been aware of it too much. The one thing I have to say about the FBI—there were several threats on Cesar's life, and they would call us and say, "You've got to get out of town. Someone's trying to kill Cesar." But they would never tell us who. And they knew who. And it was not one time, but several times, that they would call and say, "Cesar's got to get out of town right away."

ROB: Can you explain to me why, when Franklin Roosevelt signed the National Labor Relations Act in 1935, he gave all American workers the right to organize in unions, except farm, airline, railroad, and government workers?

DOLORES HUERTA: Well, it was really the Congress. The Congress made the law and the president signed the law. The reason is—we mentioned a while ago about racism? One of the officers of the Farm Bureau Federation—I think his name was Jack Angel, but I'm not sure—in a press conference in San Francisco a reporter asked him, "Why were farmworkers left out of the National Labor Relations Act?" And his answer was, because farmworkers are Mexicans and coloreds. So it was a straight racist reason.

ROB: How do you feel about that?

DOLORES HUERTA: Well, I think it's sad, because it means that today farmworkers are still so far behind, and relegated to all this poverty, even in California, where we've made a lot of progress. And you have other states, like your state, the Southern states, that still don't have the laws that cover unemployment insurance or workers' compensation. These are protections that workers have had for seventy years. And farmworkers don't have them. But I have to add this too, that the way that the National Labor Relations Act is today, it does not protect farmworkers, and it barely protects other workers, because the law has been so watered down.

ROB: Did it seem kind of ironic to you when President Clinton gave you the Eleanor Roosevelt Human Rights Award?

DOLORES HUERTA: No. Again, it wasn't the president. Franklin Roosevelt signed that law, but it was the Congress that passed it. And it was the growers that pushed to pass that law. And in fact, in 1986 I believe it was, they barely passed the law that employees had to have *toilets* in the fields! And the Farm Bureau opposed it!

ROB: That's nuts.

DOLORES HUERTA: Yeah. This is a law that we had in California in 1966. I negotiated that into the first union contracts. And we had it as part of state law in California in the 1970s. And even today, pretty much, you don't have toilets except where union contracts insist on it.

ROB: Tell me a little bit about being a contract negotiator. I know you've done that since the very first strike, which was settled in 1965. I imagine that you had to meet with a lot of high-priced white male lawyers. You'd never done anything like that before. Why were you so successful then, and continue to be so successful?

DOLORES HUERTA: Well, I think one of the reasons I was successful is because, on a personal level, when I was growing up I was very active in Girl Scouts and different church organizations, and starting my own organizations.

But then I was also a lobbyist for the Community Service Organization. So I did all the work in Sacramento. And as part of that work, since we didn't have lawyers, I would go down to the state law library and I would look up the language of the bills. And I was also very good at reading, because I like to read a lot. And I would take my proposed bill to a legislator where they would finish it up.

And so I did a lot of the work as a lobbyist, and that prepared me and gave me experience.

ROB: I know that you are very proud of your eleven children. I've heard that among them there is a doctor, a lawyer, a teacher, a public health specialist, as well as a poet and a filmmaker. A lot of kids my age don't get along with their parents and don't respect anything their parents do or believe in. Did that happen among your kids?

DOLORES HUERTA: In spite of the fact that they were very neglected, I think we get along pretty well. Naturally we have some differences of opinion, and as you get older you find your kids tell you what to do, instead of you telling them what to do! You know? And they always go through their teenage cycles. It's a part of the natural process. It's kind of that weaning period away from your parents. You start questioning your parents' values, their behavior, everything. I think it's part of a socialization process that all kids go through. You kind of have to wait for that period of time to happen, and hope that they don't damage themselves too much in the process, and wait until it's over. But since I've gone through it with all of my kids, you kind of wait for it to happen, know it's going to happen, and just hold your breath until it's over. I think it's a natural evolution that kids disagree with their parents at the ages of fourteen, fifteen, sixteen, and seventeen, until finally they say when they're older, "Dad and Mom, you were right after all."

ROB: I've heard that you're somewhat well known among your family for losing things—wallets, keys, and papers. I even heard that you once lost a computer, and another time a piano!

DOLORES HUERTA: No. I've never lost a computer. Actually I've lost two pianos! What happened is that I was very much into jazz music, and these musician friends of mine needed a piano. And I had just bought a really nice cherry wood piano, and so I lent them the piano for their gig. And they never brought it back. And we could never find it. So someone just stole it, basically. My second piano, which was the piano I've had since I was twelve years old, I brought it down from Stockton to Delano. All the retired Filipino workers lived in this place called the Agbayani. It was a labor camp, but we made it a little village for the retired Filipino workers. Most of them were single because they weren't allowed to marry in the United States because of this law that we had here. And so I put the piano there so people would come and play for the retired brothers there. And then we built a brand-new camp for them, which is in Delano, and when they were moving their stuff over to the new facility, again, someone stole my piano! And I found out who stole it, but I didn't find out until about ten years ago (this happened way back in the seventies).

ROB: This was especially interesting to me because Yo-Yo Ma, another one of my heroes that I interviewed, told me that he once left his cello in a taxi.

DOLORES HUERTA: Sometimes you have your mind preoccupied with other things. I'm always leaving my purse somewhere, and people have to say, "Hey. You left your purse." Because you're not thinking about your possessions as much as you're thinking about the next thing you're going to be doing, or the people that you're with.

ROB: I know that you speak fluent Spanish. From what I can tell, both of your parents were born in this country.

DOLORES HUERTA: So were my grandparents.

ROB: Really? So, it probably wasn't spoken in your home.

DOLORES HUERTA: It was. Oh, definitely.

ROB: So, is that where you learned it?

DOLORES HUERTA: Yes. My grandfather and my grandmother were bilingual. My parents were bilingual.

ROB: That's pretty cool.

DOLORES HUERTA: Yeah. My grandfather didn't want us to speak English, because he said English was the language of liars, because an English word can mean five different things, right? And Spanish is a very precise language. He said that the people who spoke English didn't have Spanish *palabras*. They couldn't *speak* the word, and so they had to write everything down to make sure that people didn't lie. You had to write it down. In his time—and he grew up in the late 1800s and early 1900s—a man's word was all that he had. If you didn't keep your word, there was nothing worse. That was your most precious possession. People had to be able to trust you.

ROB: It really bugs me when I read contradictory things about someone. And I've noticed it with every person I've interviewed. You'll find five completely different things. For example, some places report that your mom owned a hotel in Stockton, and some say that she took care of it for some friends who were Japanese-American and were forced to go to a relocation camp during World War II. Would you please clarify for me which it was?

DOLORES HUERTA: Actually, one thing that is true, that I've noticed a lot, is that because my mother was a woman, and she was a businesswoman, and a very progressive woman, it's hard for some people to accept that. So they always kind of diminish what my mother did. She owned the hotel. She owned the business. She didn't own the building. She leased the building and owned the business. Before that she had a restaurant that she ran. But during the Japanese relocation these friends of hers were being relocated, and so she took over the business from them, but it was her business.

ROB: You remind me a lot of my grandmother. She's very firm in her beliefs. I think she's almost ninety and she runs this store all by herself. She will accept help from her family, but that's it. She is still up there twelve hours every day. It's nuts.

DOLORES HUERTA: That's great.

ROB: I'm not saying that it's not because she's a woman, but she does it all by herself. OK. Who are your heroes now?

DOLORES HUERTA: Cesar, of course, is one of my heroes. The gentleman who got me involved in organizing—Fred Ross Sr. People like

Eleanor Smeal of the Feminist Majority Foundation, Jane Fonda, Gloria Steinem, Nancy Pelosi. People like Danny Glover [laughs], you know. Nelson Mandela, Barbara Lee (she's more like a friend). These are people that I really look up to.

ROB: You said that you were guided by two pieces of advice that you got when you were small. First of all, every action that you take, think of its impact fifty years from now. And second, your mom taught you that when you see something that needs to be done, especially if it's someone that needs help, you help them. And you don't expect any compensation or reward for what you've done. What you're doing is a reward in itself. Is there any other memory or thought from when you were my age that has been really important in your life?

DOLORES HUERTA: Don't take money from strangers [laughs]. As a child, when you're a little kid, and people try to give you something, you don't accept it without your parents' permission. That's what the rule is—don't accept anything from anyone. A lot of little kids are seduced that way. Unless your parents say you can have it, then you can't have it. You don't accept gifts. And that's interesting, when you think about that as a philosophy as you get older. It's kind of insulation against corruption.

The way the union worked, without people getting paid, you have so many good people that get bought off. You know? The whole concept that people giving you things can corrupt you. There's a big seduction there. It's something that maybe a lot of our politicians need to learn, right?

And then when you do something, you don't do it because you expect a favor in return. You do something because it's got to be done—because of the necessity there, not because you're expecting to get something in return for it.

You learn those rules when you're real small, and you don't really understand the significance of what you're being taught until later on in life. But I look back and I say, "Well, those were insulations against corruption." And it gives you a really good feeling to know that you can't be bought off, you know?

The other thing my mother taught me is to always be myself. In all of these questions, asking me about being a lobbyist or going into negotiations or whatever, always just be yourself. You don't have to pretend you're somebody else. A lot of times people hold back because they think, "Well, I don't know how to act." You don't have to worry about that. Just be yourself. And people have to accept you the way you are.

The other thing I learned, too—of course this was later on in life—never be ashamed of who you are or what you are. Especially kids of color. There's so much pressure on you to be other than what you are. Be proud of what you are.

ROB: I know this has kind of been answered, but do you believe in God?

DOLORES HUERTA: Oh, of course. We couldn't do the kind of work that we did without having faith. You have to have faith, because you're going into strange waters, so to speak, and you don't know what's going to happen. So you have to have a lot of faith.

ROB: What do you want to be doing twenty years from now?

DOLORES HUERTA: Be alive [laughs]! I'll be happy to be alive. And to be able to contribute in some way. I don't know, in ten years from now, what I can do. Like when I was sick for a whole year and a half, I couldn't do very much. I was just hoping I could get well.

ROB: What was it like?

DOLORES HUERTA: To try and learn how to walk again, how to talk, how to eat, because I ate through tubes for many months. This happened just in the years 2000 and 2001. And I'm very grateful I was able to get well and contribute some more.

ROB: If you had just one thing to say that would live on after you're gone, what would it be?

DOLORES HUERTA: I think I would say that we all need to contribute to justice in one way or another, to make the world a better place. That's got to be it. It may be in big ways or little ways, but that's got to be part of what we do while we're on this earth. To end the racism and the violence and the wars and the sexism. That's what I would want to say.

ROB: All right.

DOLORES HUERTA: I thought your questions were excellent. I don't think you needed the interview—you did so much research. It was so excellent. How far along are you in this project? How many interviews do you have to do?

ROB: I just have a few more to do. My mom and my dad help me a lot with the book.

DOLORES HUERTA: Well, congratulations. Will you publish it?

ROB: I have a publisher lined up. I just need to finish it and get it in to them.

DOLORES HUERTA: I'm glad you had a good time while you were out here, and I hope we didn't put you out of your way by not meeting with you on Saturday.

I've been out of town and just got home Friday night, and I've been gone for three weeks. And I needed to get ready for Easter because the family was getting together. So where were you yesterday?

ROB: I don't even know where we were. My older brother, Spencer, wanted to head home early, so we went in to Long Beach so he could fly home. Then we drove from there to here last night.

We spent most of the day in Mexico. A few years ago my mom and dad and I went into Mexico to buy our prescription drugs, because they are so much cheaper down there, and we didn't have any medical insurance, and yesterday we went back to the hotel we had stayed at, and had a lot of fun.

DOLORES HUERTA: That's good. I'm glad you had some fun. I felt bad—He came all this way to talk to me? And then I had to put you over until today. Thanks for coming.

13

Jackie Chan

Jackie Chan was born on April 7, 1954, in Hong Kong. His parents had recently emigrated from mainland China because of all the political upheaval there. They named their baby Chan Kong-sang, which means "Born in Hong Kong" Chan. They called him Pao-pao, which is Mandarin for "cannonball." He must have looked like a round cannonball to them, because he weighed twelve pounds when he was born—almost twice as much as most newborn babies weigh.

Chan actually went through several names before settling on Jackie. It seems to be part of the Chinese culture that your name is chosen to reflect your life and can change as your life changes. For example, when Jackie Chan started school at the Chinese Opera at age seven, his name was changed to Yuen Lau to honor his teacher's name, which was Yuen. Then when he had his first starring role in a movie in 1971, he became Chan Yuen Lung (or Long—it can be spelled both ways). Later, when he was in the movie *New Fist of Fury*, he was billed as Sing Lung. Then still later, when he lived as a young adult with his parents in Australia, he was known as Paul, then Steve, then Jack, and finally Jackie. Later in his life he discovered that his true birth name wasn't Chan at all, but Fong Si Lung. His father had changed his last name from Fong to Chan during the hard years in China.

Jackie Chan's parents were lucky to find work in Hong Kong. The city was filled with refugees fleeing from the Cultural Revolution, and there were not enough jobs to go around. The Chans worked for the French ambassador to Hong Kong. Mr. Chan was the cook and handyman in the household, and Mrs. Chan was the housekeeper. The Chans lived in the back of the embassy, by the kitchen and laundry room, in a small, windowless, bare room. Jackie's father built them a set of bunk beds, and the parents slept together in the top bunk, while their little son Jackie slept below.

Jackie Chan's father firmly believed in physical fitness, and he began training his son in Northern-style kung fu at the young age of four or five. In the Chinese culture kung fu is very important. There are many different styles of it, and the proud heritage of China's long history is reflected in it. His father's goal in teaching Jackie Chan kung fu was to teach him *how* to fight so that he wouldn't ever *have* to fight.

It was a frustrating experience for Jackie Chan when he was old enough to start school. He attended a very fine school with the other children who lived in the embassy's neighborhood. But young Jackie hated being shut up inside all day. The lessons bored him, and he had no interest in learning what was taught in school. He continually misbehaved and was sometimes punished by having to spend hours in the school's hallway holding a desk over his head.

Jackie Chan has said of those early years at school that the most useful thing he learned was how to sleep while standing up. He didn't learn to read well, nor did he succeed in any of the other academic subjects. In fact, school was such a disaster that after just one year his parents allowed him to stop attending.

Jackie's father took a job in Australia when Jackie was seven years old, leaving Jackie and his mother in Hong Kong. His father had doubts that just one parent, his mother, could control Jackie, and so the family finally decided that Jackie Chan would attend the Beijing Opera School. He would board there, and train for the Chinese Opera.

Chinese Opera is an old and traditional Chinese art form. It is somewhat like a circus or magic show in its format, and it retells very old stories about Chinese heroes. The performers had to be masters at all aspects of Chinese martial arts. They studied sword fighting as well as theater makeup, singing, stage combat, gymnastics, acting, and mime. It was vigorous training and had to be started early in a child's life. At a young age a child would be apprenticed to the Opera School, and then he lived at the school for at least six days a week. The Chinese Opera was a prestigious thing to be involved with, and families were pleased to be able to give their children this opportunity. It seemed to Mr. and Mrs. Chan that this would be a good solution for their son, and they took him there several times to see if he would be happy there.

Finally Mr. and Mrs. Chan signed a long contract with the school. The contract transferred guardianship of their son to the school for ten years and gave the school, among other things, the Chans' permission to discipline Jackie, "even to death."

Once Jackie Chan was a student at the Beijing Opera School, it became obvious that the picture created for his father was not an accurate representation of the school. The line about discipline in the contract suddenly made more sense. The students were routinely awakened at five A.M. and immediately went up on the roof to run laps. After running for a while they had breakfast, which would be a thin rice cereal called *congee*. Then they would have five or six straight hours of practice, working on acrobatics, footwork training, and martial arts. There was no restroom break until after lunch. The master of the school believed that if the children were working hard enough they would sweat away all their "toxins" and wouldn't need to urinate. So if a child asked for a bathroom break it was an indication that the child needed to sweat more, and the teacher would arrange for him to work harder and longer. Being hurt or sick was viewed the same way; the best treatment was to "sweat out" the germs by having the child work harder and longer.

Lunch at the Beijing Opera School was a more substantial meal than breakfast and was followed by many hours of "flexibility exercises." Chinese Opera performers were known for their amazing aerial acrobatics—flips and somersaults in the air—and for being able to do complete leg splits both while on the floor—horizontally—and while holding the leg over the head—vertically. Learning to do all this was very painful. The room would be filled with screams and howls. If a child couldn't do the splits completely, older children would be sent over to climb on top of him and force him down. This practice went on for hours and was agonizing for the children.

Finally the students would divide into groups to do chores or for singing or weapons instruction. After that came dinner, unless the master decided that the children needed more practice, in which case meals would be missed and the practice sessions extended.

After dinner the children were supposed to receive academic instruction. Unfortunately, they didn't really learn much. Then there would be a final session of kung fu, or face painting, or how to use opera props and costumes. Bedtime was midnight, and the next day started again at five A.M.

During a typical day at the school, the children practiced more than twelve hours. Any mistakes would earn the child a caning. Jackie Chan considered it a good day if he had not been beaten. This was the schedule seven days a week.

Jackie Chan was not the best at any of the many subjects taught at the Opera School, but he was competent in all of them. That worked in his favor, in a way. If he had shown real talent in one area, his training would have centered on just that area. Instead, he was able to learn to do everything. And he learned to do everything well.

While Chan was working so hard to become an opera performer, the art form of Chinese Opera was slowly dying. People began preferring to go to movies instead of the opera. The kung fu movies made in Hong Kong were becoming famous all around the world. By the time he graduated from the school, at age seventeen, there were no jobs to be found in opera. Many of his older "brothers" from the school had found work being stuntmen in movies, and that is what Jackie Chan did also.

Things went well for Chan in movies for a while, but two years after he started in the movie business the Hong Kong film industry dried up, and Jackie Chan couldn't find work. He joined his parents in Australia when he was nineteen. He went back and forth between Hong Kong and Australia a few times, always trying to get a break into the movies.

Chan finally got the chance he wanted, and he signed his first contract as an actor in 1976. The contract stated that for the next eight years he would make movies only for that production company. He would be paid four hundred dollars a month and would have no control over what parts he played or what movies he appeared in. The contract gave the production company the power to veto any decision in Chan's life—even whether or not he could get married.

Jackie Chan had gotten the job through the influence of Willie Chan, the general manager of the new production company. Though their last names are the same, the two men are not related. It was the start of a long friendship, which still continues. Willie Chan is currently in charge of all of Jackie Chan's businesses, and Jackie Chan insists that Willie Chan is the reason that Jackie Chan is a star today.

Slowly Jackie Chan was allowed to do the kind of movies that he admired. He had always loved the art of Buster Keaton and other early movie stars who combined comedy and action and who always did their own stunts. That was the seed for the "Jackie Chan style."

As time went on, Chan was allowed to be his own stunt coordinator, using the same stunt team repeatedly so that they all worked well together. He often directed his own movies so that his vision of how the movie should be would be carried out successfully. He worked hard to make good movies that appeared effortless. For example, one shot in *The Young Master* had Chan kick an electric fan into the air and catch it with one hand. He shot that scene five hundred times until he got the whole thing just right. His movies became known for having "super stunts"—really dangerous stunts that no one else would dare to do.

Another of his trademarks is running some of the outtakes of the movie during the closing credits. They show some of the stunts that didn't work out perfectly. They also prove that Jackie Chan uses no stunt doubles, no special effects, and no blue screens. Soon Jackie Chan was the biggest movie star in Hong Kong, and then in all of Asia—and there are three and a third billion people in Asia!

Over the years Chan has suffered some horrible injuries. He has had brain surgery in Yugoslavia; he has broken bones repeatedly all over his body. He's dislocated many bones and has suffered tremendous burns in the course of making his movies. He has had to battle his own fear of the risks he takes. In the movie *Project A*, the big stunt ended with Chan climbing up a flagpole. Then he was to jump to the top of a clock tower and drop from the face of the clock to the earth—more than fifty feet below him. There was a series of awnings that he would hit and go through, one at a time, to slow the speed of his drop and prevent him from falling straight down and being killed. When they tested the stunt using a bag of dirt, the bag exploded.

When it was time for Chan to do the stunt, the cameras rolled as he hung from the huge clock hand. He didn't jump, and finally he asked a stuntman to help him back inside the clock tower. The next day he tried the stunt again, but again he had to be pulled back inside. Day after day he tried to work up the courage to do the jump. Finally, on the seventh day, Chan instructed the stuntman to go away from the tower, so that he had no choice except to do the stunt, because no one would be around to help him back into the tower. So Chan did the stunt. And it went well. But he had to repeat it three more times to get all the camera angles that he wanted.

No one is willing to insure Jackie Chan's films because of all the risks he takes. Chan himself pays the cost of any injuries that happen on the set.

Even though he was the biggest star in Asia, Chan wanted to make movies in the United States as well. Two times he came to the United

States and made films, but neither film built on his unique strengths, and each time he returned to make more movies in Hong Kong.

In 1982 Chan married Lin Feng-jaio, who had been one of Taiwan's top actresses and was called the most beautiful woman in Taiwan. They tried to keep the marriage secret. When rumor of it finally got out, a young girl in Japan killed herself by jumping in front of a subway. Another girl in Hong Kong took poison. Chan had always thought of himself as an action-film star, but apparently his fans considered him a romantic leading man as well. A year after the marriage, their son, baby Jackie, was born. Jackie Chan and his wife are still happily married.

Finally, in 1994, the movie *Rumble in the Bronx* proved to audiences in the United States what an amazing actor Jackie Chan is. Now he is the biggest star not only in Asia but a major star in the United States as well. He continues making movies that stretch the possibilities of stunts and combine comedy and action. His character always seems to be some variation of an average person who is forced into violence by a need to protect some innocent person.

Chan is a one-man movie industry. He often produces, writes, and directs his movies as well as starring in them. Regularly he is the stunt coordinator as well. He has his own stuntmen's association and his own model and casting agency, and he has created companies to improve the technical quality of Hong Kong movies.

There are many reasons why I chose Chan as a hero. I think that the way he has risen above his abusive childhood is inspirational. I love his discipline and courage in making incredible stunts. His regular routine for keeping his body in such top shape is extraordinary. Just one example is that Chan does push-ups with one finger. And on days when he is doing just a light workout, he exercises with a hundred pounds of weight on either side of the barbell. That is for a *light* workout! But, mostly, I love the generous nature that Chan has. Over the years he has given millions of dollars to different charitable organizations. He is a loyal friend who repeatedly remembers and helps his friends and Opera School family. And he brings enjoyment and hope to millions of moviegoers, including me!

How Rob Got the Interview

I watched a documentary on Jackie Chan about five years ago that outlined what his childhood had been like and how he had persevered and risen to the very top of his profession to where he is today—the biggest movie star in the entire world. I was very impressed by the documentary, so I read Chan's autobiography. It was a great book, and it convinced me that he was a real hero, in addition to being a real celebrity.

So I started writing letters. I wrote to the producers of his movies, and I searched out some of the businesses that he owns and wrote to the managers. I wrote to some of the charitable organizations that he has helped. I wrote to every single lead I could find on any of the websites about him. I even called the Disney Company when he was working with them on *Around the World in Eighty Days* and tried to bluff my way into talking with someone who would help me contact him. It didn't work. I called a big hotel in Hong Kong, thinking that I could speak with someone who understood English, and asked them to please look up the phone number of the JC Group (Jackie Chan's main company) for me so I could call them. They told me that they couldn't find the company listed in the phone book. I wondered if that could possibly be right, but I guess I'll never know.

Amazingly, however, I actually heard back! I got an e-mail from someone in the JC Group. I have no idea which letter had actually made its way to this gentleman. He was very gracious and polite. He said that Jackie Chan loves children and would love to help with this project, if only he had time, which he did not.

I corresponded back and forth with this man for several months. Whenever I heard that Chan was going to be in the United States I'd write and remind him that I could meet Chan any place in the United States, wherever he was, and would take up only a half hour of his time. Eventually, however, this man stopped answering my e-mails. I guess I had worn him out.

I gave it a rest for a few months and then tried again. I wrote directly to Willie Chan, who is the president of the JC Group and has been a very close friend and adviser to Jackie Chan for thirty years. This time I heard back from a different man, Solon So. Again, he was very gracious and polite and regretted that Chan was not available and would not be available in the foreseeable future.

At this point I figured that it was a lost cause but that I would continue to e-mail Solon So every six weeks and just remind him that I'd still like to do the interview. I hoped that six weeks was long enough that I wouldn't totally alienate him by bothering him too much.

Imagine my astonishment when I received an electronic Christmas card from Jackie Chan, Willie Chan, and Solon So! It felt great! So I wrote back to So to thank him, and I mentioned that everything for the book had to be turned in to the publisher in five weeks, so this would be the last time I'd be bugging him for an interview.

Two days later I received an e-mail from Willie Chan congratulating me for my perseverance and inviting me to Las Vegas to interview Jackie Chan the next week! I felt euphoric.

The next week my mom, my brother Jake, and I drove to Las Vegas. Chan was appearing at the largest trade show in the United States, so there were no hotel rooms available in Las Vegas for less than five hundred dollars a night, and the prices went up to several thousand dollars a night. Fortunately, we were able to find a reasonably priced room for one day only, the day before the interview, and we decided we'd just leave after the interview so we would not have to pay for a second night's hotel room.

The day of the interview started with a trip to Radio Shack. I felt pretty dumb, but on the way to Las Vegas I'd realized that I hadn't brought the charger for the cell phone, and I had brought the phone down with just one-third battery power. Jake and I called the hotel front desk and found that there was a Radio Shack just down the street. So we found the store and ended up paying more for the charger than I thought it was worth, but, oh well.

When we got back to the hotel, my mother reported that Willie Chan had called to say that we were going to do the interview, and we needed to get there right away. So we changed into our dress clothes and quickly checked out of the hotel.

The drive over to the Las Vegas Convention Center was hectic, to say the least. We were cut off left and right. We got lost several times.

It was impossible to find a parking place, so Jake and I decided to go into the Convention Center and find the XaviX representative while my mother went to park the car.

As we entered the hall the mass of people in there overwhelmed Jake and me. We realized how incredibly hopeless the situation was. We had been told to look for a person in a black shirt with "XaviX" written in white across the front, or a person in a white shirt with "XaviX" written in black. The problem was, in either case, there were tens of thousands of people there wearing black shirts or white shirts, so it was almost impossible to see if there was anything written on their front, much less read it.

After ten or twenty minutes of searching, we decided to split up and continue looking for the XaviX person individually. The problem with this plan was that we had no way to contact each other once one of us connected with the representative. Jake didn't have a cell phone, and he didn't know the number to mine.

We remained separated for the whole rest of the interview. Luckily, I had the cell phone, and after another ten minutes of looking, Joel Talbot of XaviX gave me a call. He said, "Where are you?" and I told him I was up by the press room. He asked where that was, and we proceeded to plan to meet near the escalator. It took us a few more minutes, even though we were standing right next to each other, to finally track each other down. The number of people there still amazes me. After we turned around and recognized each other, Willie Chan introduced himself and Joel Talbot and asked where my family was. I said that we had separated to search for the XaviX representative. They asked how long we had been there, and I replied, "About forty-five minutes." And we continued with small talk as we walked toward the entrance. They said, "Well, let's go do the interview." I said, "But I can't get in—I don't have a pass to the trade show." They said, "That's OK. Just stick with us." We walked past the admissions people and onto the floor of the Convention Center itself.

The size of the room was mind-blowing. And the XaviX booth was pretty much at the center of it. When we arrived, after about a five-minute walk through the crowds of people and past huge electronic displays, I was led to a back room that had been created by using the display panels of the booth as its walls. There was Jackie Chan—just standing there.

He introduced himself and handed me a bottle of water. Chan asked what I would like written on the top of it. I suggested *R* for Rob, and he wrote that on the top. All around the room were water bottles with other initials on them. I guess Chan believes in keeping everybody well hydrated. So there I was—alone and on my own for my interview with Jackie Chan.

By pure luck, I was carrying the bag with the camera and tape recorder in it. Jake had started out carrying it because it would be his job to take photos of me with Chan and monitor the tape recording. I don't know at what point I started carrying it, but I was awfully glad I had it! We proceeded to start the interview. As Chan was answering the first question I realized that I hadn't turned the tape recorder on, and I had to stop him while I got that going.

About a third of the way through the questions I was hoping to ask, Willie Chan stepped in and said, "I'm sorry, but ESPN is here to do their interview. Can you wait and come back in twenty minutes to finish yours?" I said, "Sure, I'll be happy to come back," and I began to pack up the camera and tape recorder, but Jackie Chan said to leave my things. I asked if it would be all right for me to go out and look for my family. And that is what I did.

I left the booth and ran, literally sprinting and dodging through crowds of people, jumping in and out of booths. I think Jackie Chan might actually have been proud of me. When I finally got out of the trade show area into the front area, I looked around for about thirty seconds and didn't see them. I saw the time and realized that it had taken me five minutes to get out there, even though I had given it my all. So I started running back but was stopped at the entrance to the exhibit area. They wanted to see my admission pass. Of course, I still didn't have one. I explained to the guards that I was in the middle of an interview with Jackie Chan but had been interrupted by ESPN and that if I didn't get back there it would be on their heads!

The guard said, "You're doing an interview with *who*?" I said, "Jackie Chan." She asked, "At which booth?" I explained that it was at the XaviX booth and that I was in the middle of the interview and really had no time to stand there and explain it. And she said, "All right. Go ahead." It was amazing that she believed that a sixteen-year-old kid was having an interview with someone of Jackie Chan's stature. But I'm glad she did!

I sprinted back to the XaviX booth, managing to get lost twice on the way and taking about seven minutes total. I ran up horribly worried and out of breath, but, luckily, the demonstration that Jackie Chan was doing for ESPN was still going on, and so I was in luck.

As I waited there for Chan, I decided to call my home in Salt Lake to see if they had heard anything from my mom or Jake as to where they were. But they'd had no word. As I was about to hang up, one of Chan's assistants found me and said, "Oh, there you are. Jackie Chan is waiting for you!" So I hung up immediately and went in and apologized for being late to finish the interview. I got some great pictures and headed out of the Exhibit Hall, where I found Jake and my mom standing anxiously by the outside door.

———◆———

Interview

INTERNATIONAL CONSUMER ELECTRONICS SHOW, LAS VEGAS, NEVADA, JANUARY 6, 2005

ROB: Thank you so much for making the time to speak with me. Your movies have given so much pleasure to my whole family and me all my life. Even my little brother, who has Down syndrome, loves to watch your movies and your animated television show. And I really appreciate your making time to talk to me. I know that your schedule must be very busy.

JACKIE CHAN: That is very true. When I look at my schedule, there's not one day to rest. When I'm making a movie, we work seven days a week, nonstop, because any time an American production calls me, I have to go. And then there is coming back to promote the film and the junkets. We are not even talking about going back to China to help the charity things. I'm happy, but I wouldn't mind having a vacation right now. For me, a vacation would be eight whole hours of sleep!

ROB: As you know, my book is about what my heroes' lives were like when they were about my age (basically from ages eleven to sixteen, which is when I've been working on this book). You've talked about the Beijing Opera School. It sounds pretty gruesome. I know that you were caned for not performing well enough, and not given enough time to sleep, and made to work for eighteen hours a day. Your nature is to be very optimistic and happy-go-lucky. Did you feel that way during those years?

JACKIE CHAN: While the training in the Opera School was hard, we were a family. As a family we were very optimistic once we kids were alone, without any of the teachers around. We were very happy, and we played together once we were alone.

ROB: At the Institute all the students slept together on the same rug, which was filthy dirty and soiled with urine. You were sleep-deprived. Food was withheld if you weren't progressing fast enough in your training. Illnesses went untreated because you didn't dare report feeling sick because then the master would make you work even harder to "sweat" the fever out. There were regular beatings and long hours of painful exercises. In spite of all that, you ended up in wonderfully good health and with a strong body. Were you just lucky, or how did that happen?

JACKIE CHAN: I think I have always been lucky. But the hard work and discipline trained our bodies to be tough.

ROB: How many children were there in the Institute at one time? I know that you began performing very early and also had your first part in a movie when you were just eight years old.

JACKIE CHAN: There were from about thirty to fifty students at a time.

ROB: Who were your heroes when you were about my age? Are they still your heroes today? What would they think of what you have accomplished with your life?

JACKIE CHAN: My heroes were mainly the policemen, the firemen, the people who were serving the people. At one point I dreamed of becoming a fireman. I still believe that those are the real heroes, and they are the people who deserve to be idolized and respected, not movie stars.

I don't think that I should be considered a hero. I'm just Jackie. I'm still human.

ROB: I know that you watch your diet and eat very healthy foods, mostly vegetables. It seems strange to me that you market a soft drink. How did that happen?

JACKIE CHAN: What are you referring to? [turns and speaks in Mandarin for a minute with Willie Chan] Do you mean my commercials for Mountain Dew?

ROB: Yes, and also in Asia a soft drink called "Bobo Cha."

JACKIE CHAN: The Mountain Dew ads are all about exercise and getting outside and doing things. That's the reason I could feel good about endorsing them. Because it's about exercise.

For me, exercise is very important. If there is an opportunity for exercise, I'll take it. For example, if I can walk up three flights of stairs, I'll walk up three flights of stairs rather than taking an elevator.

ROB: You have broken many bones, burned the skin off your hands, had brain surgery, broken your nose three times, had a tooth kicked out, and dislocated your hip, among other bones. You've said that you are always in pain. When my brother interviewed Florence Griffith-Joyner for this book, she said kind of the same thing—that she was looking forward to becoming an actor because it wouldn't always *hurt*. Lance Armstrong, another of our heroes, would probably say the same thing about the pain. At the same time you say how much joy the work gives you and that you do it for fun. How can both things be true?

JACKIE CHAN: My philosophy is that you do the very best you can do. As far as the stunts—I can only do about 50 percent of what I could do without even thinking about it when I was twenty. I know that someday I'll have to stop doing the action things. Maybe I can teach. But for now, it is fun to do the very best I can do and to do things that no one else will do.

ROB: I know that you don't believe in organized religion. Do you believe in God?

JACKIE CHAN: I don't have a religion. No religion at all. I just think you should trust more in your own heart. I believe more in the things that I see. And what I see is that the thing that most people have died for is religion. I don't think you should sit at home and tell the Buddha to help you have good health—no, you have to train and exercise, and then you'll have good health.

If there is a God, then He helps everybody. God is not Chinese or Japanese. I don't have to believe in Him. God helps everybody. That's my philosophy. So what I do is do the best that I can in the movie business. And a lot of other people are with me, I give them jobs. I take care of my family, then I give money to the charities. It makes me happy. That's all. I just try to help people. That's my philosophy.

ROB: You speak at least eleven languages [Korean, Mandarin, Shandong, Shanghai, English, Cantonese, Japanese, Taiwanese, Spanish, some French, some Thai] learned mostly while you spent months in different countries shooting movies. Which language do you dream in? Count in? Read books for pleasure in?

JACKIE CHAN: I dream in Mandarin. I also read in Mandarin. I count in Cantonese.

ROB: You have very little education. Your mother couldn't read or write. And yet you have this amazing capacity to learn languages, to master all the knowledge you need to own and run many different businesses. How has that happened?

JACKIE CHAN: Just a little bit at a time. For example, when I starred with Chris Tucker in *Rush Hour*, I didn't really know him and I was hiding from him. When he came to talk to me I would just hide from him because I didn't understand English very much, so I didn't know what he was saying and I had to respond. But my English was not good enough, so how could I respond? So, I'd hide in my motor home and only see him on the set. Slowly we would get to know each other on the promotion tours. In Japan, Hong Kong, and Korea we stayed together, we ate together, and [we] became good friends. Now we are buddies.

What I learned I learned mainly from social interaction. The Chinese have a saying that goes, "It is better to travel one thousand miles than to go to school for one year."

ROB: Your love for all people of different races and different circumstances is very obvious. You spend a lot of time and money helping other people. I read just this weekend that you've already contributed half a million dollars to the tsunami relief work. I just want you to know that I appreciate that you try to promote peace and be a positive role model in your movies.

I've asked my other heroes what their favorite books were when they were my ages. Did you have any favorite books when you were my age? I've read that you like science fiction now, as do I. What are some of your favorite books now?

JACKIE CHAN: I didn't have very many favorite books when I was your age or younger because I didn't have much time to read. The time that I might have been reading I slept, or I relaxed because of the intense training I was getting at the Institute.

My favorite books now are about Chinese history. I love historical novels and explanations about Chinese history.

ROB: You promised your dad, when you were young, that you would never join a gang, gamble, or use drugs. Many people start abusing drugs while treating painful injuries. And you've certainly had much more than your share of injuries! How have you avoided having that happen to you?

JACKIE CHAN: The Institute taught us all to respect our bodies. The teachers there educated us about the dangers of drugs and taught us respect for our bodies. It was part of the discipline that I learned at the Institute. It was just something that you didn't do. So it has never really been an issue for me. It was just trained and bred into me to such an extent that I never considered using drugs.

ROB: I know that once you were out of the Institute, when you were about seventeen, you enjoyed bowling and playing pool. What were some of your other interests then?

JACKIE CHAN: When I first got out of the Opera everything was new to me—there was a whole new world out there! I learned that I liked soccer very much. Then I learned and liked boxing. People were always introducing me to new things. But I loved pool. I would play it almost twenty-four hours a day.

ROB: At about the same time you were in some real street fights, and you've said that you saw people killed. Did those experiences influence your decision to move more into comedy and spectacular stunts and away from so much fighting in your movies?

JACKIE CHAN: I hate violence, but I like action. It's a real dilemma. I really hate a really violent movie. They are really disgusting. So now in my movies I always tell children good things. All my movies have some message. That's my philosophy. We have a responsibility to do something positive for society. We should show bad things on the screen as little as possible, because we are the role models.

ROB: Who are your heroes now?

JACKIE CHAN: Sylvester Stallone. He's been my hero for a long time. I admire him because he writes the script, he directs, he acts, and he does everything. I admire people who have talent and it's not just that you are handsome. Handsome—there are too many handsome men and pretty girls every year. Talent keeps your career forever.

Movies like *Tuxedo* are what I want to be doing now. More acting with some special effects, and with my own action, and more acting and drama. Because I don't want to be an action star. An action star—their life is so short. I want my life to get longer. I want my career to be longer.

A few years ago I tried to make a movie with Stallone. He wanted to do *Rambo IV*. He wanted me to be a drug dealer. But a *good* bad guy—starting out bad, but later on becoming a good guy. But all my fans wrote me letters saying, "No, you cannot be a drug dealer." So I know I cannot do a drug dealer.

They aren't heroes exactly, but Donald Duck and Dustin Hoffman have been inspirations for my underdog character in some of the movies. Hoffman, he's not very tough, but people like him.

ROB: In 1999 you discovered that you have two sets of half brothers and sisters in China. Did you feel betrayed when you found out? Have you formed a relationship with them now?

JACKIE CHAN: I didn't feel betrayed. Actually I respect my parents more because of what they did. My parents went through unimaginable hard times in China during World War II and afterward. They were able to get out of China to Hong Kong, but they were not able to bring their families with them. I respect them for always sending money and letters back to their children.

I will continue to respect my parents.

————————